final
sale

The Studio Book

The Studio Book

Melba Levick

Photography

Kathleen Riquelme

Text

UNIVERSE

First published in the United States of America in
2003 by Universe Publishing
A division of Rizzoli International Publications, Inc.
300 Park Avenue South, New York, NY 10010
www.rizzoliusa.com

ISBN: 0-7893-1007-4
LCCN: 2003104963

Designed by Judy Geib and Aldo Sampieri

Printed and bound in China

2003 2004 2005 2006 2007 / 10 9 8 7 6 5 4 3 2 1

To my son, Bret, with love —M.L.

To my husband, John Quisenberry —K.R.

Page 2
Walls of steel-troweled stucco enclose the sculpture garden in Charles Arnoldi's
Venice compound.

Page 5
A view of San Francisco and a private beach are among the amenities in the
Pt. Richmond studio of Gregory Ghent and Xtopher Seldon.

Page 12
Renowned architect Bernard Maybeck lived in this Berkeley home from 1923
to his death in 1957.

Page 14
Charles Green, half of the Pasadena architectural team of Greene and Greene,
moved permanently to Carmel in 1922. He began construction on his studio
the following year. The used-brick and tile studio features an arched entry and
elaborately carved teak door. Photograph © 2003 Radoslaw Kurzaj.

Page 15
Charles Green's original studio space, with its imposing 12-panel skylight, has
been lovingly restored and furnished by Green's son and daughter-in-law.
Photograph © 2003 Radoslaw Kurzaj.

Page 16
Hawk Tower in Carmel was completed in 1925 by poet Robinson Jeffers.

Page 19
Nestled in a courtyard and enveloped by wisteria, the Meridian Studios were
once part of Santa Barbara's 1830 Lugo Adobe. Architect Bernard Hoffman
remodeled the estate in 1922, converting two of its wings into artists' studios
that remain occupied to this day.

Page 22
The studio of the landmark Pacific Palisades home of designers Charles and
RAy Eames is now used as a business office. In the foreground is the iconic
Eames lounge chair and ottoman, which evolved from the couple's design for
molded-plywood splints commissioned by the U.S. Navy during World War II.
Photography by Tim Street-Porter. Courtesy of the Eames Office.
© 2002 Lucia Eames.

Page 24
The interior of Julius Shulman's studio, taken in the fifties by the acclaimed
photographer. Built in 1950 by Raphael Soriano, Shulman's steel-framed
studio, across the courtyard from his house, remains a thriving hub of activity
and a treasure trove of architectural history. Photograph courtesy of
Julius Shulman.

CONTENTS

INTRODUCTION 8

BEACH BUNGALOWS AND A POOL 26
The Billy Al Bengston Studio

AN ABANDONED POTATO CHIP FACTORY 34
The Charles Arnoldi Studio

HISTORY AND A PRIVATE BEACH 40
The Gregory Ghent and Xtopher Seldon Studios

A PLACE TO REGROUP AND CREATE 46
The Roseline Delisle Studio

HOMAGE TO VAN GOGH IN ARLES 52
The R.B. Kitaj Studio

AN EVERYMAN'S CASTLE 60
The Roger Herman Studio

FOR A MASTER VIOLINIST 68
The Jascha Heifetz Studio

AN OJAI RETREAT 74
The Beatrice Wood Studio

AN ECLECTIC STUDIO
AND A
MINIMAL STUDIO 82
The Elena Siff and Sam Erenberg Studios

FRANK GEHRY'S FORMER OFFICE 88
The Manfred Müller Studio

A WOODWORKER AND A CHICKEN COOP 94
The Sam Maloof Studio

DESIGNED ON A PAPER NAPKIN 100
The Robbie Conal Studio

GLASS PANELS FRAMED IN WOOD 106
The Alice Corning Studio

HIGH CEILINGS, LIGHT, AND A CUPOLA 112
The Ed Moses Studio

"A CASE STUDY BEACH SHACK" 122
The Tom Schnabel Studio

ROOM TO WALK AROUND 128
The Harrison Houlé Studio

TWO STUDIOS 134
The Studios of Nathan Oliveira

AN OASIS OF INCONGRUITY 142
The Woods Davy Studio

A SQUARE AND TRIANGULAR SPACE 148
The John McCormick Studio

BROKEN BENCH BINDERY   154
The Gail Sulmeyer Studio

**"EARTHQUAKE-PROOF IN A
CONTRARY WAY"**   160
The Art Carpenter Studio

ONCE A "RAMSHACKLE FARMHOUSE"   168
The Laura Cooper and Nick Taggart Studio

A DOWNTOWN LOFT   174
The Fred and JoAnne Balak Studio

"MY SHIP AT SEA"   180
The Fletcher Benton Studio

NORTH LIGHT AND A POOL   188
The Hubert Schmalix Studio

SIMPLIFICATION AND LIGHT   196
The Huguette Caland Studio

SPACE FOR A PHOTOGRAPHER   204
The Julius Shulman Studio

A FORMER CARRIAGE HOUSE   214
The Kate and Odom Stamps Studios

FIRE, EARTHQUAKE AND MUDSLIDE   222
The Kim McCarty Studio

**RE-IMAGINING A MEDICAL-ARTS
BUILDING**   228
The Simon Toparovsky and Randy Franks Studios

A BARN AND A GARAGE   234
The Kurt Ernest Steger and Libby Hayes Studios

AMONG ORANGE GROVES   240
The John Nava Studio

MEDITERRANEAN VILLA WITH A VIEW   246
The Miriam Wosk Studio

A SAN FRANCISCO ROW HOUSE   254
Tjasa Owen Studio

ENTHUSIASM FOR THE TROPICS   260
The Robert and Lorri Kline Ramirez Studio

TOR HOUSE AND HAWK TOWER   272
Robinson and Una Jeffers' Studios

ACKNOWLEDGMENTS   282

INTRODUCTION

I nitially the word *studio* was used to describe the work itself rather than the workplace. Derived from the Latin word for *zeal*, it connotes the passion with which an artist pursues his work. Over time the word's meaning ventured from the act of creation to the place where creation itself, in all its many manifestations, takes place. Today the studio is acknowledged to be a space of many shapes and forms—in essence a conception as varied as the individuals who think up, work in, and inhabit them.

At turns, studios are well ordered and messy, welcoming and forbidding, forthright and shrouded in secrecy. One constant, however, remains: a studio is a laboratory for creativity, an inspired repository in which an individual strives to reinvent or refocus the world around him.

In medieval times the studio was not the province of one individual but home to a large collective or workshop filled with artists and craftsmen toiling in anonymity. From there it evolved into Renaissance *estudiolos*, which frequently doubled as miniature museums, whose enlightened occupants were breaking out of obscurity and developing prestige and position in society for the first time.

After the "artist" ceased to be regarded as a tradesman and came into his own in the early 1800s as an individual called to a "vocation," art academies sprang up to teach technique and the first private artists' studios appeared. The best of the lot ranged from simple working studios with ample space and light to grandiose showplaces of society painters that were jam-packed with art and expensive objects. Less conventional artists broke away from the academies and took up residence in makeshift work spaces, which were located typically wherever rent was cheap and space was available.

At the turn of the twentieth century, Paris was still the art capital of the world, replete with academically trained artists and young iconoclasts. Artists flocked to the City of Light from around the world, most with little money. They tended to congregate in Paris's seedy bohemian enclaves, such as Montmartre, where artists would occupy any inexpensive room they could find. At this time, there also existed a type of European studio for the better heeled. Traditionally this was a high-ceilinged space with one or two walls of angled windows, which allowed for an abundance of light, preferably from the north.

This concept of the artist's studio was carried to America in the late 1800s and early 1900s, and often took the form of the showplace Manhattan studio, popularized by the likes of society favorite William Merritt Chase. He kept "court" and held gala receptions in his lavish Greenwich Village studio in the historic Tenth Street Studio Building at 51 West 10th Street, a hub for wealthy artists.

During the 1930s urban lofts came of age in New York, replacing the more elegant European studio in the public's mind as the artist's place of work. These bare industrial spaces were carved out of former factories in rundown sections of the city.

New York artists were battered by noise, crowds, and inclement weather. Thus, many creative individuals sought a more salubrious climate and moved west—a good number of them to California. There, enthusiastic writers and artists discovered in their adopted state an Edenic land of temperate weather, gentle winds, sunshine, and myriad economic opportunities. As opposed to the urban ills found in the dystopian East, California was seen as a domestic ideal, dotted with front lawns and friendly bungalows.

In postwar America of the 1920s and 1930s, California benefited from a steady stream of European émigrés whose influences would be felt in all of the arts, particularly architecture and design. Yet years before the arrival of such early modernist icons as Rudolph Schindler and Richard Neutra, California functioned as an incubator for the likes of such American giants as Bernard Maybeck in Northern California and the Greene Brothers to the south.

Maybeck was a visionary, one of the true originals in American architecture, who seamlessly blended classical and vernacular styles. Born in New York in 1862, he went to Paris at age nineteen and trained at the prestigious École des Beaux Arts. Upon finishing his studies, he returned to the U.S., ultimately settling in California in 1890, where he was most prolific from 1900 to 1915. The architect had no one distinct style and took advantage of the new century's many achievements, freely revisiting the past when it suited him. Employing large windows, Maybeck brought light into interiors, and he integrated living areas and gardens. As well, heavily influenced by the Arts and Crafts movement, he was moved to explore the opportunities inherent in redwood interiors, handcrafted detailing, and hand-wrought fireplaces.

Although Maybeck had three different studios in San Francisco over the decades, he spent his later years working in his Berkeley house (page 12). It is fitting that, in keeping with the architect's love of gardens and the outdoors, landscape designers now live there.

The Arts and Crafts movement, which rejected the Industrial Revolution and emphasized handcrafting, indigenous materials, and a connection to nature, thrived in California at the turn of the twentieth century. One element of the philosophy was the promotion of a harmonious and healthful living environment. The bungalows in this spirit were low-slung, integrated into the landscape, and constructed of wood with hand-wrought ornamentation.

Maybeck, in the Bay Area, followed the tenets of simplicity and economy in his designs. In Southern California, however, the style, under its chief proponents Charles and Henry Greene of Pasadena, became much more lavish.

The brothers started their architectural firm of Greene and Greene in 1893, and together they pioneered a fresh and indigenous style of architecture that epitomized the relaxed and outdoor-oriented way of living in California. This lifestyle suited their wealthy clients, many of whom were from the weather-challenged Midwest.

After World War I, Charles was eager for a change and by 1922 he had withdrawn from the firm and taken up permanent residence in Carmel, on the Monterey Peninsula. The quaint and

picturesque ocean-side village was promoted as an artist colony at the turn of the century. Following the San Francisco earthquake of 1906, it became a refuge for many Bay Area writers and artists, who built cozy cottages and cabins among the spectacular landscape.

It was 1923 when Charles Greene was able to begin construction on his own studio in Carmel. Built of used brick recycled from the demolition of a nearby hotel, it was unlike the large wood residences he had built for clients. Work was scarce from this period on, and Greene passed his days in the studio writing, holding music recitals, and leading discussion groups on Eastern philosophy and religion (pages 14 – 17). The studio has been enlarged and is maintained by its present occupants, Greene's son and daughter-in-law.

Around the same time that Charles Greene was completing his studio, renowned poet Robinson Jeffers was finishing Hawk Tower, a place for writing and reflection for his wife and family, adjacent to their Carmel house. Miraculously, Jeffers managed to build the 40-foot-high structure by himself, hauling up huge boulders from the beach, "making stone love stone," as he described the process in his poetry (page 18).

Farther south on the coast, in the historic community of Santa Barbara, building styles were derived from Spanish and mission architecture. The town, too, became a popular place for writers and artists. In 1922 architect Bernard Hoffman remodeled the 1830 Lugo Adobe, which had belonged to one of Santa Barbara's wealthiest Spanish families, and converted two wings into the Meridian Studios, which are still occupied by artists and architects to this day (page 21).

After World War II, California experienced an economic and population surge due to burgeoning defense, shipbuilding, and aerospace industries. New materials and technologies developed during the war could now be adapted to housing. Mass production and standardization kept costs down. A prescient Los Angeles editor and publisher named John Entenza, of *Arts and Architecture* magazine, attempted to address the challenge of postwar housing with his Case Study House program. He enlisted a group of well-known architects to produce two-bedroom houses that were affordable and easy to maintain. The architectural precepts included open plans, flat roofs, a minimum of internal walls for greater spatial flexibility, and a blurring of the division between house and garden. Perhaps the best known and most influential was the Pacific Palisades house and studio of Charles and Ray Eames, created from industrial and off-the-shelf components by the legendary design team. While much of their design work took place at their office in Venice, the couple relaxed, incubated ideas and made a film, *Toccata for Toy Trains* (1957), in their home studio (at present used as a business office)—now considered a modernist classic (pages 22 – 23).

While the Case Study House project firmly established Los Angeles at the forefront of architecture and a new kind of casual suburban living, it would not have gained its worldwide recognition without the aid of award-winning architectural photographer Julius Shulman. Shulman photographed California masterpieces by the likes of Neutra and Schindler, as well as Case Study houses. And to this day he continues to live and work in a Hollywood hills house and studio designed by Case Study architect Raphael Soriano in 1950 (page 24). Both structures have been designated Cultural Heritage Board Monuments.

From the turn of the twentieth century, California has had a profound architectural history, a history since complemented by great achievement in the other arts. This, coupled with the abundant beauties of the natural world and a general attitude of optimism and excitement, has fostered an environment of great attraction for a variety creative people—all of whom have visions of that perfect space in which to bring their own ideas to life.

To this day, whether designed by internationally renowned architects or not, studios remain bastions of individual expression and incubators of creativity. California, with its temperate climate and healthy iconoclasm, is an ideal environment in which to live, work, and dream. The studios in this book are exemplars of this spirit.

BEACH BUNGALOWS
AND
A POOL

The Billy Al Bengston Studio

Although he was born in Dodge City, Kansas, artist Billy Al Bengston is the quintessential Californian. At age 15 he arrived in Los Angeles, where he became enamored of surfing and ceramics. In spite of a spotty college career he attended art school in both Northern and Southern California, benefiting from teachers such as Richard Diebenkorn, Nathan Oliveira and Peter Voulkos.

He was in the right place at the right time in 1957, when L.A.'s sputtering contemporary art scene got a jumpstart with the opening of the now-legendary Ferus Gallery. Bengston had his first solo show there the following year and gained fame as one of the forerunners of the "L.A. Look."

While serious and self-disciplined in his art, Bengston's wilder side came out in motorcycle racing, rough-water swimming and surfing, images that would resonate in his work. His vivid colors and depictions of irises and palm trees spoke to the light and tropical flavor of his adopted home. In fact, Bengston relates that while he was in London to exhibit a series of paintings influenced by California and Mexico, he was shocked at how garish his work appeared in the foggy, dank British capital. "It was like the circus had come to town," he says.

Water has played a huge role in his life and art, and water is one of the first things one notices (and almost falls into) upon arriving at Bengston's colorful, rambling house and studio complex in Venice, with surfboards lined up against bright blue walls. Back in the early 1980s he purchased seven rundown beach bungalows, built in 1911, and an adjoining abandoned potato chip factory with artist Charles Arnoldi. (They split the property when Arnoldi married.) Evidence of an era of looser building codes remains. The complex is composed of a series of structures—some new, some refurbished—that encircle the large lap pool. One small bungalow contains the kitchen and living room; a second the bedrooms; another his daughter's playroom or "office," as Bengston calls it. However, the largest and tallest structure is the artist's second-story studio he built from scratch, complete with an outdoor

painting studio and an office/library and adjoining garage underneath.

Indoor/outdoor living is mandatory for Bengston. Even before the studio was built the pool went in. "I have my priorities," he quips, as he surveys his property from his studio deck. And as testament to his early real estate involvement and Venice's fame as an artists mecca, a host of pricey loft-studios have sprung up in place of once-empty lots and derelict buildings. "When I first moved here there was gunfire every night," recalls Bengston. But everything mellows with age, including Venice and one of its favorite sons. The laid-back artist now has the time to appreciate his good fortune and play the family man, as well as nurture his new love of gardening. "In 1960, none of us artists in California knew if we could make it as a career without having another profession. I guess I was a leader for others in saying that I was going to be an artist for a living whether I died of it or not."

The Billy Al Bengston Studio 33

AN ABANDONED
POTATO CHIP FACTORY

The Charles Arnoldi Studio

Nearly twenty years ago, friend and fellow artist Billy Al Bengston told Charles Arnoldi that "artists don't own real estate." After quickly realizing the error of his statement, Bengston teamed up with Arnoldi to purchase a half-acre of dilapidated Venice property for their joint living and working areas. While Bengston has remained a Venice resident and has built his own studio on his part of the property, Arnoldi has moved his living quarters to a contemporary oceanfront house he designed for himself and his family in Malibu. His creative life, however, still revolves around the cavernous 12,000-square-foot compound of painting and printing studios, sculpture garden, and exhibition and conference spaces he carved from an abandoned potato chip factory back in the early 1980s.

Arnoldi, a tireless tinkerer, continues to add new structures and modify existing ones. "If I want anything, I build it," he says. "The studio's changing all the time." Adjacent to the kitchen off the sculpture garden, for example, is his former dining/living room that has been reconfigured to serve for client meetings and to display work. The old potato chip warehouse comprises his painting and printing studios. Although Arnoldi laments his building's "dungeonlike" atmosphere, he admits he found it impossible to work in his ocean-facing home studio in Malibu. To compensate for the closed-in feeling, he's added skylights along the spine of the ceiling and imposing metal roll-up doors for light, ventilation and access.

His compound's ongoing renovation goes hand-in-hand with the artist's love of "playing with space." Arnoldi's appreciation of space and materials was evident in his design for DC-3, a celebrated restaurant at the Santa Monica Airport, and these talents are lauded by architect Frank Gehry, his good friend and former work neighbor on the Venice Boardwalk in the 1970s.

Yet along with Arnoldi's love of space is his appreciation for the lack of space, especially in Los Angeles. "My ideal studio would be on a giant plot of land," he says somewhat wistfully. But, admitting the impossibility of that dream, for now he'll keep experimenting with the one he has.

HISTORY
AND
A PRIVATE BEACH

The Gregory Ghent
and
Xtopher Seldon Studio

Owning a studio that has both history and a private beach is a luxury most artists only dream about. For sculptor Gregory Ghent, moving into his house and adjoining studio in Point Richmond "opened the door for art. I had never worked in such a concentrated way before," says the former gallery owner, art appraiser and collector. Ghent now shares the two-story studio with digital artist Xtopher Seldon, making them the third generation of artists who have lived and created there.

In 1930 the painter Worth Ryder, a prominent member of the UC Berkeley art department, and his friend and colleague, artist John Haley, purchased two adjoining lots on the San Francisco Bay in Pt. Richmond. They built two identical, side-by-side, two-story studios in the European style, with a prominent bank of north-facing windows on the upper story. Five years later Haley and his wife, Monica, added living quarters to the downstairs of their studio, while Ryder, who lived in Berkeley, used his solely for painting. When Ryder died in 1960 the Haleys purchased his studio for Haley to use, and the couple further renovated their property to make room for exhibition space for their extensive collection of African, Oceanic and indigenous art.

The Haleys became friends with Ghent through the latter's San Francisco art gallery, and hired him to inventory Haley's artwork as well as the couple's art collection. Ghent also wrote the catalog for a Haley retrospective after the artist's death. When Haley's widow died in 1997, the couple's collection and their real estate were left to Ghent, who now serves as a protector of the Haley legacy.

A few years ago, Ghent advertised for a live-in caretaker/carpenter to help maintain the property. Seldon, an ex-contractor and architecture student, "found the ad almost too good to be true." After moving in, Seldon, too, felt the pull of the studio's history. "I was inspired by Haley's breadth of work and his openness as an artist," says Seldon, who lives and works in the studio's second floor, formerly used for storage, that he renovated. "I've made a serious commitment to be an artist," says the self-taught artist, who also paints and does assemblage.

Ghent produces and fires his table-top nudes in the studio's first floor and occasionally works from models in the light-filled second story, which features doors that slide open to reveal the spectacular view of the bay and the lush, terraced sitting areas and patios. Ghent lives in the Haleys' former home—"That little walk to the studio does make a difference," he says of his separate workspace—where he also holds receptions and exhibitions of his work and collections as well as those of Haleys. "The fact that these spaces were built by artists and that artists still live here is unusual for California," Ghent says. "I feel responsible for maintaining the legacy."

A PLACE TO REGROUP AND CREATE

The Roseline Delisle Studio

When she first arrived in Los Angeles a quarter-century ago on what was supposed to be a two-week vacation, Quebec-born ceramist Roseline Delisle barely spoke English and hardly knew a soul. But as a woman who spent every summer of her youth living in the wilderness with her father and siblings, such minor obstacles as lack of fluency and friends were not going to stand in her way. "I said I came to Los Angeles to see if oranges grew on trees, but I really meant that I couldn't imagine a place where there was no snow, no cold," says Delisle. "I came here for the exoticism, but L.A. was not as exotic as I thought. Immediately I felt I belonged."

Upon arriving, Delisle met a woman in Venice who was loading a kiln and looking for someone to sublet her ceramics studio. After Delisle looked up **sublet** in the dictionary she agreed to take over the lease. She quickly gained a reputation for her flawlessly crafted, boldly colored porcelain vessels. Yet in tandem with her growing fame was the escalating rent on her studio. So, after marrying painter Bruce Cohen and purchasing a 1926 Spanish bungalow in Santa Monica, she brought her studio home. With the help of her artist friends she converted a "filthy garage-turned-woodshop" into an airy, white "room of my own, a place to regroup and create," says Delisle, looking out to the surrounding yard and garden.

The first order of business was to create a level surface upon which to place her wheel. She covered the existing concrete floor with wood. Then drywall and skylights were installed. Delisle salvaged the windows from Otis Parsons, the art school where she was teaching, and she retrieved the sinks from the trash. The painted cabinet was purchased from the former office of Charles and Ray Eames, which had been down the street from Delisle's Venice studio. Then, to make the room feel lighter and larger, she removed the ceiling joists and replaced them with cable. The studio is entered through a beveled-glass and oak door that was a wedding present. Another entrance is through the alley, essential when Delisle receives her half-ton orders of clay.

One important change that has been made since the studio was created in 1990 is the addition of an adjoining

mini-studio. Originally intended as either a garden shed or storage, it has evolved into a workplace for Delisle's eight-year-old daughter, Lili. Another change came with Lili's birth. Suddenly, Delisle's work grew. Her small nonfunctional porcelain pieces gave way to nearly lifesized vessels. To effect this change in size, the artist needed to change mediums, switching from porcelain to earthenware. In a sense it was an artistic rebirth after giving birth.

These elegant large shapes take on a decidedly human presence. Some are reminiscent of Balinese dancers with cone-shaped hats, nipped waists and full skirts. In fact, Delisle often groups the boldly striped, black, white and bright blue pieces together, forming what she calls a "family with personality."

Family is an important concept for Delisle, and her work is a recurring subject in her husband's paintings. "His works often show small vases and vessels," says Delisle of her husband's romantic gesture. "The problem is, people often want to buy what they see in Bruce's paintings. So I guess I'll keep making some small pieces, too."

HOMAGE
TO
VAN GOGH
IN ARLES

The R.B. Kitaj Studio

Artist R. B. Kitaj has been identified with his adopted city of London for so long that it's a surprise to find him now living in the village of Westwood, just blocks from UCLA. He returned to Los Angeles in 1997 after his wife Sandra died suddenly of a brain aneurism. Kitaj, who sees himself as a man of many identities—expatriate American, Anglophile and diasporic Jew—and who frequently alludes to the theme of displacement in his work, has finally come "back to the bosom of my family," he says. In fact, his whole clan lives within five doors of the artist.

His house, with its painting studio fashioned from a garage, was one of just a handful of homes he looked at in the area. His teenage son liked it best, so Kitaj bought it. The artist's interests lie in books and art, not furniture and decoration. Thus, the only alterations to the home were the addition of bookshelves throughout and tack board on the walls of the living room, which he has transformed into his drawing studio. The most extensive remodeling was reserved for the former garage. L.A.-based architect Barbara Callas, of Callas-Shortridge

Architects, was responsible for the renovation. "Kitaj was very busy in London getting ready to move back to the States, so we did most of the design on the phone or via written communication," recalls Callas.

"I told Barbara to just open up the garage. I didn't care how large it was," says Kitaj. "In London there is a different style of living. Artists like [Francis] Bacon and [Lucien] Freud work in tiny crowded rooms. Only in America do we yearn for these great spaces," he adds.

The most striking alteration to the garage was the exterior paint, a chrome yellow Kitaj chose as an homage to Van Gogh's house in Arles. "I also liked the contrast with the swimming pool," he adds. Inside he requested tack board walls and clerestories that admit the prized northern light. "That's what every artist wants, but I've never had it before," remarks Kitaj. He opted to leave the gears on the garage doors because he likes how they look, even though he never opens them. Kitaj is that rare Angeleno who doesn't own a car. "Everything I need is within a few blocks," he says.

Like his house, Kitaj's studio is filled with art and books—and not much furniture. The Mies daybed was a housewarming gift, but "I never sit on it," Kitaj remarks. He's too busy completing a series of paintings that depict Kitaj and his late wife as angels. "When Diebenkorn came to Los Angeles he painted the community of Ocean Park," says the artist. "Hockney discovered swimming pools. But I found the idea of man and woman."

And, speaking of Hockney: the two old friends, who both enrolled at London's Royal College of Art on the same day in 1962, are once again living in the same city. "However, when David and I get together now we don't compare drawings—we compare hearing aids," says Kitaj.

AN EVERYMAN'S CASTLE

The Roger Herman Studio

Artist Roger Herman is known for his large-scale, colorful work—a description which also suits his Los Angeles home and studio. Created in collaboration with local architect Frederick Fisher, the imposing edifice was built in the late 1980s on a strangely shaped lot that abuts a park near Dodger Stadium. Clad in plywood which Herman has stained a bright green with vibrant blue trim, the towering three-story structure stands in sharp contrast to the neighborhood's squat prewar bungalows.

One enters through a ten-foot-high door, built to accommodate Herman's many large canvases, and into the cavernous studio, with its fourteen-foot, exposed joist ceiling. Recently the painter, printmaker, ceramist and professor of art at UCLA divided the studio into two discrete areas. By adding walls and a gargantuan ochre pocket door, he created a front "office," which also contains vitrines of his ceramic bowls, and, behind it, the larger, higher-ceilinged studio. "I needed a more private space in which to work," says Herman.

Although the house and studio overlook hilly parkland, Herman blocked out the windows in his studio—not because of the distraction the view caused but because of his need for even light. "The sun was impossible," he says. "I can control the artificial light. And, anyway, I work a lot at night."

Herman's home and studio were creatures born of collaboration and necessity. What determined the shape were the three contiguous lots the artist purchased a few years prior to planning the house. "The lots form a triangle, so the house echoes the shape," he says. For the German-born artist, who came to Los Angeles in 1980, space was a priority. His first residence in the city was a 10,000-square-foot warehouse downtown. "I have never lived in an apartment, so I needed room," he says. Economics, too, played a part in the design. Fisher created a no-frills space using low-cost materials such as plywood, Douglas fir and drywall, and incorporated the large industrial windows Herman had salvaged from downtown buildings. Then Fisher tweaked Herman's

original concept, and added a third-floor master-bedroom tower. The result could be called an everyman's castle.

Architecture and domestic interiors are often featured prominently in Herman's prints and paintings. Yet when he moved into his new studio, he experienced a painting block. "I freaked out because everything was so clean and freshly painted, so at first I worked in the garage," Herman recalls. In time, however, he got comfortable and even painted the varnished plywood floor white after he found the dark color too distracting.

Soon Herman's studio will become part of a Hollywood tradition—the sequel. The artist is once again collaborating with Fred Fisher on a new two-story studio next door to his existing one. Only this time around some changes will be made: the structure will be clad in metal and feature a lap pool in back. Welcome to L.A.

FOR A MASTER VIOLINIST

The Jascha Heifetz Studio

Aesthetics and acoustics were given equal weight in Lloyd Wright's 1947 design for the Beverly Hills home studio of master violinist Jascha Heifetz. Wright, son of iconic architect Frank Lloyd Wright, had already built a house for the violinist a decade earlier in Newport Beach, south of Los Angeles. So, when Heifetz moved to a hilltop Beverly Hills house, he commissioned Wright to make minor alterations to the house and build a studio, to be connected to the residence by a breezeway.

Heifetz and Wright were a good fit. The violinist's austere personality and well-documented perfectionism were reminiscent of the younger Wright's father. And the architect's profound familiarity with music and acoustics were crucial when creating Heifetz's studio. Wright had constructed two acoustically superior shells for the Hollywood Bowl in the 1920s. He also designed houses for many of the area's celebrated musicians such as cellist Gregor Piatigorsky, who often performed with Heifetz at the Bowl.

For Heifetz's studio, Wright created a trio of hexagonal spaces, including two smaller spaces—one serving as the entrance hall, the other as the secretary's office—with a large studio in between. Paneled in a warm

redwood, with an imposing sandstone-and-brick fireplace and surrounding seating area, the studio looked out through a bank of windows to the landscape beyond. Early in his career, Wright worked as a landscape architect, and he always strove to incorporate the outdoors into his designs.

After Heifetz's death in 1987 the house and studio were sold and slated for demolition. The Los Angeles Conservancy, an architecture-preservation organization, campaigned to save the studio. The owner agreed to donate it, if it could be moved to another site. Toby E. Mayman, at the time the executive director of the Colburn School of Performing Arts, stepped in and raised the funds to reconstruct the studio in the school's as-yet-unbuilt future headquarters.

Since its new space would not be ready for several years, the studio had to be dismantled and stored. Venice-based architect Harold Zellman, a restorer of several Lloyd Wright buildings, was hired to oversee the disassembly and reconstruction of the studio. For Zellman the project was "more archeology than architecture." He followed Lloyd Wright's original construction documents to rebuild the studio—but

first he had to take it apart. Every piece was numbered twice and documented before put into storage. "I treated it like a model airplane kit—but in reverse," says Zellman. When the Colburn School was completed in 1999, Zellman worked with the school's architects to site the studio on its second floor. There was not enough space to include the secretary's office, but everything else conforms to the original specifications.

According to Zellman, the studio's lack of opposing parallel walls and the geometry of the pitched ceilings were Wright's ways of improving upon the acoustics. Zellman maintained the acoustical properties, since the studio, as in Heifetz's time, is used for violin lessons, master classes and recitals. Also, it seems appropriate that the Colburn School, which is associated with the University of Southern California, is the studio's guardian. Heifetz's last public performance, in 1972, was a benefit for USC. The studio's site is appropriate for another reason: while its windows no longer look out on leafy treetops, it now faces the undulating curves of Frank Gehry's Disney Concert Hall, the new home of the Los Angeles Philharmonic.

AN
OJAI
RETREAT

The Beatrice Wood Studio

Colorful is an apt adjective with which to describe the late ceramist Beatrice Wood, whether commenting on her tumultuous love life, her fashionable saris, or her renowned iridescent glazes. Born into a wealthy and conventional New York family in 1893, Wood decided, at age 19, to escape to Paris and pursue the bohemian life of an artist. While studying painting, she embarked on a romance with novelist Henri-Pierre Roché, who later authored *Jules et Jim*. Wood returned to New York at the outbreak of World War I, where she fell in with the New York Dada group and into the arms of Marcel Duchamp. Her long friendship with the artist earned her the nickname "the mama of Dada."

Wood's exposure to Dadaism would continue to inspire her. As would two other experiences that affected her for the rest of her life. In 1923, at age 30, Wood met Indian philosopher Krishnamurti and became a lifelong adherent of Theosophy. That same year Wood made her initial trip to Los Angeles (she moved there permanently in 1928). But it would be a decade before her introduction to ceramics in a night class at Hollywood High. Her hobby becomes a vocation while studying with celebrated studio potter Glen Lukens at the University of Southern

California, and later with famed émigré ceramists Gertrud and Otto Natzler.

After making her home in Los Angeles for twenty years, Wood decamped to the fertile valley of Ojai, ninety minutes north of the city, where she lived and worked for the next half-century. She died at her home in 1998 at the age of 105.

The two types of pottery that solidified Wood's reputation are poles apart. Most acclaimed are her luminous lusterware pots and vessels, done with a refined glazing technique that employs metallic salts, which reflect light waves, creating an effect that breaks the light beam into dark and light bands of color. Wood's achievements in this area remain without peer. The second category involves her "naughty" figures. Humorous and playful, these hand-built pieces deal with down-to-earth subjects such as love and sex.

The ceramist's final 24 years were spent in the ranch-style home and studio she built—now open to the public—on 450 acres of the Happy Valley Foundation, a non-sectarian educational, cultural and research center, whose school was founded by notables such as Krishnamurti and Aldous Huxley. Located in the upper Ojai Valley, the house is now a showroom and gallery featuring some of Wood's extensive collection of folk art, Asian antiques and jewelry, as well as selected works for sale. Outside, in a corner of the deck, is an elaborate broken-tile "throne," an artist friend's gift to Wood on her 102nd birthday.

It was on this pillow-strewn throne where she entertained her many visitors, including writers, artists and celebrities. In fact, according to Beatrice Wood Studio Director Martin Gewirtz, one of her friends, *Titanic* director James Cameron, modeled the character portrayed by Gloria Stuart on Wood. The actress is sitting at a potter's wheel at the beginning of the movie.

And it was in the studio, with its wheel looking toward the beautiful Topa Topa Mountains, where Wood practiced her alchemy four hours a day until the end of her life. Divided into various workstations—for lusterglazing, for making figures, for hand building, and for throwing at the wheel—the studio remains much as it was at the time of her death. Tools are neatly organized on hooks; paints, chemical compounds, colored pencils and brushes are arranged at the ready. A favorite joke around town is that Ojai's fabled Pink Moment sunsets resulted from a mixture of Wood's chemicals as she tirelessly perfected her glazes over the years.

AN ECLECTIC STUDIO
AND
A MINIMAL STUDIO

The Elena Siff
and
Sam Erenberg Studios

The workspaces of husband and wife artists Elena Siff and Sam Erenberg could be right out of *The Odd Couple*. Siff, who works in collage and assemblage, has a studio a pack rat would love. A glass-walled addition to the main house, the large, light-filled, high-ceilinged room is chockablock with stuff—found objects, buttons, costume jewelry, Mexican tin pieces, old books and magazines—all the necessities of Siff's art. While there are shelves and two large tables to hold many of her materials, as well as her works in progress, the studio's organization is random at best. "Of course, *I* know where everything is," Siff says. "It's my first real studio," adds the artist, who lived with her husband in Santa Barbara for 20 years before they moved to Santa Monica. "And I'm happy to never have to clean it up. But I can close it off. That's why the door is so important."

It was a commission Siff received to create "art in the market place" at the Frank Gehry-designed Santa Monica Place mall that brought the couple back to L.A., where they had met in art school. They commuted from Santa Barbara the first year, but with their children grown they decided to plunge into the Los Angeles real estate market in 1994.

Sam Erenberg, a painter and installation artist, has always had a separate home studio due to the toxicity of his paints and, he says, "the desire to leave the house to

go to work." When the couple found their 1930 Spanish-style bungalow in Santa Monica, Erenberg opted to convert the falling-down garage into his studio space.

To handle the renovations the couple chose the noted Australian-born architects Hank Koning and Julie Eizenberg, who just happened to live down the street. Siff and Erenberg admired their residential work, and Siff liked the fact she'd be working with a woman. The couple collaborated with the architects on their studio design, but Siff chose the exterior colors. A rich red defines the new addition, which includes a master suite above Siff's studio. The bright blue wall, seen through the windows of Siff's workspace, demarcates the house's original back wall. The artist also looks out on another addition—the lap pool, whose colorful tiles she made.

Sam's studio, which is as pared-down as Elena's is jam-packed, is white-walled, featuring a large skylight and small clerestories that open for ventilation. Originally, Erenberg, whose pieces range from small watercolors to serene abstract landscapes, requested a single area to serve as work and exhibition space, but the former garage's drainage and grading problems led the architects to divide the structure into a front office/storage area and a larger studio/gallery. To increase visual interest on the exterior, Koning and Eizenberg made the stucco walls concave and clad the entrance wall in galvanized metal.

FRANK GEHRY'S FORMER OFFICE

The Manfred Müller Studio

Artist Manfred Müller was born in a city of ruins—postwar Düsseldorf, Germany, a city in great need of rebuilding. Perhaps this is one reason why architecture plays such an important role in his art and life. In fact, many of his sculptural installations have been referred to as "architectural interventions," due to the specificity of and sensitivity to their site. "There is a symbiotic relationship between architecture and sculpture. I grew up with an appreciation for the correlation between functional art and fine art, like the idea of the Bauhaus," says Müller, who first came to Los Angeles in 1989, where he was a member of a group show at the original Santa Monica Museum of Art. The museum and its surrounding commercial Edgemar complex, which was built on the site of a former dairy, were designed by Frank Gehry in 1988.

This would mark Müller's first close encounter with the work of the renowned architect. Fast forward to 1996. Müller and his wife were house hunting when a friend steered them to an industrial section of Santa Monica and a cluster of six metal-clad studios that had also been built by Gehry. The unit the couple purchased turned out to be Gehry's former office.

However, the pared-down three-story structure was, to misquote Le Corbusier, a machine for working in, *not* living in. Just a small mezzanine on the second floor separated the first two stories, and there were no interior walls to define the spaces. No matter. Müller, with a penchant for power tools and a love of woodworking, set about turning the space into a serious studio and a welcoming home. "A large space is important to me. I need to be challenged by it," he says. His white-walled and light-filled studio now boasts an eighteen-foot-heigh ceiling.

To solve the storage and partition problems, Müller built elegant maple cabinetry that is flexible and multipurpose. Most of the pieces are on wheels so that closets, shelving and cabinets can be relocated and reconfigured at a push. The solid birch dining table—also built by Müller—doubles as a work/exhibition area for his thousands of paper pieces, among them vibrant blue- and red-painted felt paper sculptures folded like coats and collages that Müller calls "footnotes," which contain references from his large site-specific installations.

Los Angeles is responsible for his seemingly boundless output. "The accessibility of materials and the energy of

America make it possible," Müller enthuses. His permanent public installation, *Twilight and Yearning* under the Santa Monica Pier, is a love letter to California. The effect of the work, which consists of three red boats strapped to pilings, changes with the tides.

Naturally, Müller still has ties to the city of his birth. He has maintained a studio for more than two decades in a former factory in Düsseldorf, which he visits frequently. The city of ruins is no more. Just a mile from his studio, a sprawling cutting-edge commercial and cultural center has sprung up along the waterfront. Called Der Neue Zollhof, it was designed by none other than Frank Gehry.

A WOODWORKER
AND
A CHICKEN COOP

The Sam Maloof Studio

People magazine dubbed him the "Hemingway of Hardwood," and the MacArthur Foundation awarded him a "genius" grant, but master wood craftsman Sam Maloof eschews these lofty titles. "I'm a furniture maker, I'm a woodworker, and I think *woodworker*'s a very good word . . . an honest word," he says. The 87-year-old Maloof, who was born just miles from his current home in Alta Loma, didn't train to become America's foremost furniture maker and creator of presidential rocking chairs. It was a dearth of well-designed, affordable furniture that gave impetus to his career.

Maloof was working as a graphic designer in 1948 when he met and married his wife Alfreda. But after settling into a tiny tract house, the couple couldn't find anything suitable to put in it. Having made some pieces for a previous apartment, Maloof now set about furnishing the entire house. A friend then contacted *Better Homes and Gardens*, which published a laudatory feature on the home's interiors. The rest is history.

He traded the equity in his home for a shack and a bunch of citrus groves in nearby Rancho Cucamonga, and installed his workshop in a ramshackle chicken coop. In time he laid the foundation for his home and studio and then just kept on building—both his

business and his landmark house and workshop, which now comprise 8,500 square feet and 26 rooms. Initially, though, time was in as short supply as storage space. "There was never enough room," he recalls. From the beginning Maloof's clean-lined, timeless and ergonomic furniture garnered praise and orders. His career choice was surprising for this son of Lebanese immigrants. "The Lebanese don't like to work with their hands," he remarks with a smile.

Not one to follow trends, Maloof blends form, function and beauty in his work and his home. He's fortunate to have lived and worked surrounded by family, and he enjoys the camaraderie of a trio of loyal assistants— including for a time his son, Slimen, who now has his own workshop on the property. His hand-built home is an ever-changing gallery in which to display his handiwork and furniture, as well as the collections of American Indian pottery, rugs, dolls and baskets he amassed with his late wife. Notable touches are the distinctive latches on every door and a magnificent hand-carved spiral staircase.

Yet, in the late 1990s, his house, workshop and five-acre site were threatened with demolition when the state gave permission for an addition to a freeway that

would run right through his property. The only way to protect his home and workshop was to move both structures and declare them landmarks, listing both on the National Register of Historic Places. They were dismantled piece by piece and transported to a nearby site at the foot of the San Gabriel Mountains, where the Sam and Alfreda Maloof Foundation was set up as a cultural center and museum. "It was heartbreaking to watch the buildings being taken apart, but now it seems like they've been here forever," says Maloof. "However, it's kind of spooky. The house orientation is exactly the same but the surroundings are somewhat different." Nevertheless, everywhere Sam Maloof looks he sees something he's created, an achievement he credits to God. "I feel He uses my hands as tools. I hope in some way I've been able to give part of this blessing to others."

DESIGNED
ON
A PAPER NAPKIN

The Robbie Conal Studio

Painter and self-styled "guerilla artist" Robbie Conal has been lampooning America's political and corporate honchos with his posters since the Reagan Administration. But he is firmly planted in the 1940s when it comes to architecture. About a decade ago he and his wife, graphics designer Deborah Ross, bought their home, which was built by renowned architect Gregory Ain in 1948 as part of a fifty-house, two-and-a-half block housing project in the Mar Vista neighborhood of Los Angeles. For years Ross worked out of a section of their bedroom, while Conal toiled in a studio converted from the previous owners' garage-turned-master-bedroom—a dark, blue-shag-carpeted "love shack," as Conal describes it. When Ross expanded her company and moved to larger quarters, it was time to rethink Conal's working environment.

The couple was adamant about honoring the spirit of Ain's architecture in the new studio. Ross, who was inspired by a 1938 studio Ain had built for a cinemato-grapher, sketched out a preliminary design on a paper napkin. ("All our best work is done on the kitchen table," quips Conal.) An architect friend then turned the drawing into a rendering for their contractor to follow.

The process took four months. They remodeled the "love shack" and extended it by several feet, adding some height and west-facing clerestory windows for

light and ventilation. The result is an expansive white-walled 900-square-foot studio bearing the couple's signature touches. Two bright-yellow sliding doors—whose handles are hood ornaments from a '48 Studebaker and a '51 Chevy and Mercury—allow access to and from the carport as well as the patio, where Conal often paints outdoors. The sliding doors honor Ain's modular building style and echo their home's flexible walls.

Conal added movable, hanging halogen lights on parallel cables, because "they look cool" and "turn the studio into a great presentation space for art," he remarks. He also followed two important tips given to him by an artist friend: include as many electrical outlets as possible, and sheer all walls with extra plywood so works can be hung anywhere in the studio.

The colors were Ross's department. She chose yellow because "it's cheerful and makes you feel good." The light green is "an homage to the home's original avocado-green paint." And the periwinkle blue trim "blends with the sky and lifts the roof," she adds. A corner of the studio is made of blue sandblasted glass that "glows like a lantern at night," reports Conal. The results are so successful that this guerilla artist sounds downright content when praising his new studio. "It's just so great," he says. "I want to work all the time."

GLASS PANELS FRAMED IN WOOD

The Alice Corning Studio

Nearly one hundred years separate ceramist Alice Corning's Mill Valley home and her glass-clad studio, but both structures share the two-acre property's million-dollar view. Corning has lived in the house—built in the late 1880s and situated on a winding single-lane road—since 1974, when she moved from Manhattan. Upon graduation from Harvard with a degree in English literature she planned on being a poet. But after taking some ceramics workshops in SoHo, "I found I wanted to create with my hands rather than with words," she remarks.

Initially Corning set up a studio in the former laundry room of her Marin County home, but she found herself longing for more space and a view of the lush landscape. "My original idea was a free-standing structure, a romantic space nestled among the trees," she recalls. However, an architect she consulted convinced her of the practicality of having the studio attached to the house, but recommended she create a contemporary studio that was separate from the home's public areas.

In spite of the compromise, Corning got what she wanted—plenty of space and light. The walls and eighteen-foot-heigh ceilings are composed of glass panels framed in wood, giving the studio a greenhouse feel. "I definitely wanted a daytime studio," says Corning. "It feels like a tree house, and it's fabulous when it rains. The sound can be deafening." To combat another weather problem, the often-powerful sun and heat, she installed electronically operated black shades.

Building the studio was a testament of woman over Mother Nature. For earthquake-proofing, the structure was framed with steel beams that had to be lowered over the house by crane. In addition to constructing the main studio, Corning converted an adjacent low-ceilinged toolshed-turned-maid's-quarters into a storage room that now contains examples of her work from the last thirty years. Corning had wooden-lipped shelving designed to hold the pieces—a design that passed the earthquake test with flying colors.

Light wood accents abound, from the flooring to the built-in storage to the custom shelving, both to add warmth to the space and because Corning loves the way they look. Wood and glass doors lead to a spacious deck (there is another deck on top of the studio off the living room), where Corning's large gas kiln sits. Here, too, is another Corning touch—an outdoor shower. "It gets very dirty working with clay. So I have a shower nearby with a view." On the deck she can lounge on chairs, surveying the garden and the occasional deer while her pieces are being fired. "Firing can take many hours and I need to check the kiln often," she says. "That's why it's important for a ceramist to have a studio at home."

Corning holds open studios twice a year and acknowledges the benefits the studio has bestowed on her work. "Environment influences the forms we make," she says. "Pieces have emerged from here that are original and special."

HIGH CEILINGS, LIGHT, AND A CUPOLA

The Ed Moses Studio

In 1987, when Ed Moses asked architect Steven Ehrlich to build him a studio at his Venice residence, he requested a freestanding structure. "A studio is for work, a house is for living," declared the artist. Over the years, however, Moses' freewheeling creativity has led him to fuse house and studio. He built an exterior second-story balcony that connects his bedroom to a mezzanine in his studio, from which he can observe his work. He's also added a carport and a metal roll-up door to the back of the studio, which is actually at the front of the property.

Such changes, however, have not affected the original mission and sensibility of the studio. Moses requested an unpretentious and serene building with high ceilings and plenty of light. Ehrlich complied, creating a 1,400-square-foot structure, topped by a cupola, that has the simplicity of a Shaker church. Clad in plywood, now well weathered and stained green (the house is red), the interior features a double-height wooden ceiling with thick beams and trusses, and a spine of dual clerestory windows that runs the length of the cupola. Ample white walls are designed to complement Moses' large-scale abstracts, giving the space the mood of a gallery.

The Zenlike studio reflects Moses' spiritual and aesthetic sensibilities.

The Culver City-based Ehrlich, whose practice was originally in Venice, has had a long association with the area's artists. And Moses has often included architectural installations in his exhibitions. Therefore, the two were a good match. So much so, in fact, that the year after Ehrlich completed Moses' studio he asked the artist to collaborate with him on the inner-city recreation center he was building. Moses designed dynamic, patterned exterior walls of sandstone, red brick, and black blocks that remain graffiti-free to this day.

Says Ehrlich of his client and friend: "Ed always uses the phrase 'Create a little magic.' That's what I hope his studio achieves."

"A CASE STUDY BEACH SHACK"

The Tom Schnabel Studio

Tom Schnabel is a well-respected disc jockey, programmer and self-proclaimed "world-music cheerleader." He is also a former lifeguard. "I've always lived near the water," says Schnabel, who grew up in Santa Monica close to the Case Study houses of Charles and Ray Eames and Richard Neutra, which fueled his early interest in mid-century Modernism. It made sense, therefore, to combine clean lines and clear water in the design of his home office and recording studio in Venice. "Modern design has always appealed to me," he says. "I see it as a corollary to the music I like. It's clean, and it has rhythm and flow, just like jazz."

Schnabel had been living in his current Venice home for a decade before the house next door came up for sale. He asked Robert Ramirez, who designed his house, to create an adjacent office/music studio and pool. "I came up with a '50s Case Study beach shack," says Ramirez, who chose not to mimic the Spanish style of Schnabel's home. "Tom's interests in both architecture and music are eclectic. He likes modern and rustic, so I wanted to emphasize flow, openness and nature. And he appreciates things that are finely tuned."

Ramirez's solution was a stripped-down, serene space that measures twenty feet square. It is also environmentally friendly—a concern of both Schnabel and Ramirez. Solar panels on the roof allow for ambient heating. Abundant wood accents—from ceiling and roof overhang to shelving and built-ins—add another kind of warmth. Glass is also an important component. A glass door on the tiny adjoining recording studio "keeps me from getting claustrophobic," says Schnabel, as does the view through the office's window walls and French doors that open to the salt-water lap pool and spa.

The architect's predilection for the tropics is evident in the surrounding landscape and Ramirez's ever-present outdoor shower. "Bob has a hands-on approach to living and working," says Schnabel of Ramirez. "He brings a sensuality and a love of different cultures to his work."

ROOM
TO
WALK AROUND

The Harrison Houlé Studio

When artist Harrison Houlé and her new husband, actor John Schuck, built their Venice home ten years ago, Houlé made room for a 500-square-foot painting studio, located across the courtyard from the house. She included a bathroom with shower, a long sink where she could develop photographs, and arranged for abundant light. "I used skylights and clerestory windows in order to increase the wall space for my paintings," says Houlé. And she added French doors that opened to the courtyard patio. "I needed space to walk around while working," she says.

But such careful planning was disturbed when the couple moved to New York for three years, after just 18 months in their new home. Houlé and Schuck leased the house and studio to artists, and, when they returned from the East, one of the tenants wanted to continue renting the studio.

Since Houlé's husband often spends long stretches in Manhattan working in the theater, she agreed, and decided to move her studio into the front of the house. With that move, she and her art began to change. "Once I cleaned the space, I felt I could do anything I wanted to it," Houlé says. (Schuck was given his own space—the "red room"—filled with

books, desk, easy chair, television and other assorted "guy things," she adds.)

Houlé never anticipated the feeling of freedom that would accompany the change in her work environment. Her canvases grew, her energy increased, and there was a newfound spontaneity in her work. The rooms' colors, reminiscent of those in the south of France, are echoed in her paintings. "I can now work on three or four paintings at once; I can move furniture around when I feel like it, and I can be cooking and working at the same time," she says. " I think it's a woman thing. I love to be surrounded by beautiful objects and smells from the kitchen while I work."

TWO STUDIOS

The Studios of Nathan Oliveira

Nathan Oliveira considers himself a lucky man. The artist and professor emeritus at Stanford has two studios—at least for the time being.

On a hill about a mile from his house, within an imposing shingle-sided structure that the university built for his use, lies the first studio. The space is of comfortable and voluminous dimension—forty square feet with twenty-foot-high ceilings. The space nicely accommodates his sometimes very large work, including, once, his huge thirty-foot-long "Wings series" of paintings. Just beyond the walls of this studio, Oliveira has found solace on the surrounding hillside, which has provided a place of exercise for the artist and his dog, as well as the opportunity to observe nature, a prominent theme in Oliveira's work.

The second studio is an addition to the comfortable ranch-style house that Oliveira and his wife have shared for over thirty years. Having retired, now uncertain about the status of the Stanford-owned studio, Oliveira had the second studio built. Although not as large as his hilltop space, Oliveira's home studio is a comfortable space of thirty-two by twenty-four feet. "Having a studio at home is recognition of my senior

status," he jokes. "It's much more accessible. I can come in and look at paintings until the light is almost gone." An angled window wall that looks to the garden echoes Parisian painting studios at the turn of the twentieth century. "Angling is inspiration, a square box is not," notes Oliveira. To even out the light he added a corner skylight that subtly washes the wall. And the pitched ceiling and white walls increase the room's elegant spaciousness. "This is the sum of all the studios I've ever had," says Oliveira. "My previous ones were makeovers, converted, always makeshift. I yearned for what I have now."

AN OASIS OF INCONGRUITY

The Woods Davy Studio

Thinking big could describe both the work and the studio of sculptor Woods Davy. The Venice-based artist is known for his abstract pieces that combine such natural materials as stone and wood. His home and studio, by design and necessity, had to be spacious enough to accommodate his large-scale projects.

In 1986 Davy and his wife, former graphics designer Kathleen Dantini, called upon their friend, Malibu architect A. Thomas Torres, to help design their house on a narrow lot in Venice. To solve problems imposed by the lot size, Torres oriented the house on a diagonal. The couple's artistic sensibilities and the architect's expertise combined to create flexible spaces replete with imaginative angles and light sources as well as entertaining jolts of color.

The first hint of an artist-in-residence is gleaned through the corrugated metal gate that leads to the sculpture garden holding many of Davy's pieces. Davy, who does many public-art commissions, often moves his sculptures directly from the studio to the garden in order to observe them in a natural setting. The first floor was designed as a series of flowing spaces that open to one another and to the outdoors. The large

gallery dominates the downstairs. It is bookended by the kitchen/dining area at one end and a metal roll-up garage door at the other, and serves as a bridge between the studio and living room. The slate-floored gallery soars to twenty-three feet and receives abundant northern light from a grouping of clerestory windows. This lofty space has accommodated both imposing sculptures and a seventeen-foot-tall Christmas tree.

Initially, Davy planned the wide door openings off the gallery in order to enable him to drive an electric forklift from his studio right through the first floor and out to the sculpture garden. That has yet to happen, but his two daughters have done their share of indoor roller skating. "I wanted an environment in which I could represent my work myself in my home town, as well as entertain clients and host events," he says.

Throughout, the architecture creates elegant sight lines to best complement the artist's work and the couple's impressive collection of Pre-Columbian sculpture and African tribal art, which Davy feels makes connections to his own work. But it is the spacious, light-filled, twenty-six-foot-high studio

adjacent to the gallery that is the focal point of his creativity. Taking up nearly a third of the home's 3,500 square feet, the studio also features a galvanized roll-up gate that leads to an outdoor work area and what Davy calls his "sculpture graveyard." One essential for the studio was its accessibility to an alley, since the artist frequently travels to the Mexican beaches of northern Baja to handpick the large stones he incorporates into his sculptures. "The shape is the most important determinant," says Davy of his selection process. "I like to take things out of their normal context." The same could be said of his house/studio, which remains an oasis of incongruity amid the neighborhood's humble bungalows and housing projects.

A SQUARE
AND
TRIANGULAR SPACE

The John McCormick Studio

John McCormick's Marin County studio is only 500 square feet, "but what it lacks in size it makes up for in views," says the artist. His evocative, mist-filled landscapes, however, are not based on what he sees from the windows and doors of his studio. McCormick's serene works are what he calls "studio inventions." "I'm not interested in documenting nature," he continues. "My work is subjective."

Even though his paintings don't describe his immediate surroundings, the area's natural beauty is what turned McCormick from abstraction to landscapes when he moved out of San Francisco a decade ago. After he and his wife, photographer Jan Gauthier, bought their Corte Madera home, McCormick built his studio over the garage to take advantage of the lush location, working with an architect he met at one of his openings. To maintain the feeling and spirit of the original architecture, he matched the pitched roofline with that of the rest of the house. "The studio is both a square and a triangular space," he says. "It relates to sacred architecture and has wonderful energy."

It also has extraordinary light. He added a ceiling skylight and a pair of French doors, one of which opens to a small deck and views of Mt. Tamalpais and

the Pacific Ocean. Wood on the beamed ceiling and the flooring furthers the treetop feeling.

When McCormick is not working on his imaginary landscapes, he moves down the cantilevered stairs to the deck and garden one flight below, to hone the charcoal studies he characterizes as "his primitive impulse to make marks."

The artist and his works are right at home in the Bay Area, with its long tradition of landscape painting. "My artistic ecosystem is where I live," says McCormick. "It's all right here."

BROKEN BENCH BINDERY

The Gail Sulmeyer Studio

After graduating from U.C. Berkeley with an art history degree, Gail Sulmeyer married, moved to Los Angeles and took a job cataloging prints and drawings at the L.A. County Museum of Art. While there, a book collector asked Sulmeyer to catalog her private collection. "I had no idea such beautiful books existed," she says. Many were from private presses and featured exquisite paper, printing and binding. "It opened my eyes to a new world and a new vocation."

After Sulmeyer divorced and moved to the Santa Barbara enclave of Montecito a decade ago she was able to dedicate herself full-time to bookbinding. Her Broken Bench Bindery specializes in leather design bindings and custom boxes for books and artists' prints, and its large clientele has come entirely from word-of-mouth.

Happily, Sulmeyer's home came complete with a finished Victorian garret-like attic, which she has customized to her meet needs. A carpenter built the large center-island worktable with flat drawers to hold outsize sheets of paper; pegboard keeps her small tools organized and out of the way, helpful in a small space; light filters in from tilted rectangular windows that open for ventilation. Sulmeyer, though, is vigilant about covering all materials at the end of the day to protect against fading.

From the studio's front door, accessible via a long flight of stairs, Sulmeyer can survey Montecito's legendary natural beauty. Beyond her guesthouse, draped in belladonna, the majestic Santa Barbara Mountains rise up.

"EARTHQUAKE-PROOF IN A CONTRARY WAY"

The Art Carpenter Studio

Wood plays a huge part in Art Carpenter's life—from his last name to the location of his home/studio to his award-winning furniture designs. For more than forty years Carpenter has been honing his craft in the backwoods of Bolinas in northern Marin County at his Espenet Studio. (Espenet is his middle name. As he explains it: "I couldn't put up a sign that read 'Carpenter Studio,' now could I?")

The artist, originally from the East Coast, first glimpsed the San Francisco skyline during shore leave from the Navy. He never left. Carpenter's first forays into wood were turned bowls, which he produced for ten years. Then, on an outing to Bolinas with his wife and children, he noticed a sign advertising land for sale. He bought a dozen acres, and he and his family settled into a home on the property. He built his workshop and began making "furniture on training wheels," as he describes his initial designs. As Carpenter got braver his furniture got bigger, and he added on to his long narrow workshop, which is wedged between a road and a marsh, and next to the San Andreas Fault.

When Carpenter and his wife divorced she got the house but, he says, "I had too much iron in my studio to move." Thus, in 1973 he began building his new living quarters adjacent to the workshop. He added one building a year to the woodsy compound. The result is a series of geometric wooden structures nestled in the forest. Among his handmade buildings is a separate showroom, a guestroom, an office/master bedroom, a kitchen/living room combination, an outdoor privy complete with telephone, and a separate bath and shower structure. Although Carpenter has employed a variety of shapes in the creation of his home and workshop, he prefers round. "It's simpler; every wedge is identical." And in spite of the fact that he lives and works practically on top of a major fault line, his buildings are "earthquake-proof in a contrary way," he remarks. "The construction is so loose. There are no inner joints."

The woodworker, who has been proclaimed a living treasure of California, views his structures as a reaction against what he refers to as the trend toward architectural supersizing. "I call them SUV buildings," he declares. However, his downsized living

arrangement does have a downside: no excess is allowed due to limited storage space. Nevertheless, Carpenter manages to collect rugs. "They're easy to display, they don't break, and they keep me warm in winter," he says smiling.

ONCE A "RAMSHACKLE FARMHOUSE"

The Laura Cooper
and
Nick Taggart Studio

It's hard to tell where nature leaves off and nurturing begins in the lives of artists and landscape designers Laura Cooper and Nick Taggart. The couple is equally at home planting, painting and parenting. "Everything interconnects—our lives, our art and the garden," says Cooper. "Our home blurs the border between life and art."

Taggart has lived in the house in the Glassell Park section of Los Angeles for more than a quarter-century. Cooper moved in fourteen years ago. By that time love was in bloom, but the garden wasn't. "Laura made sweeping changes to the exterior," says Taggart, who discovered his green thumb as well. And the transformed landscape, viewed from his studio courtesy of a pre-existing pullout window, has had a profound impact on his art: "It informs almost everything," he says. Taggart primarily paints and draws, and his intricate black-and-white drawings feature insects and plants. Some of his thickly applied, vibrantly colored oils have a tactile quality and topographic feel.

At first nothing blocked the window, but today his studio looks out into a colorful tangle of treetops, where figs are ripe for the plucking. "It's chaotic, yet calming," Taggart remarks.

Over the years Taggart has rebuilt every room of this former "ramshackle farmhouse" and reoriented the house to the garden. A native of Devon, England, he came to Los Angeles for a visit and never left. He found in this rural outpost the perfect balance between city and country." A loft or a studio without windows would have been too claustrophobic," he says.

Upon entering the front gate for the first time, Cooper, from leafy La Jolla, near San Diego, felt as if she'd always belonged here. The overgrown foliage and the hilltop house triggered memories of *The Secret Garden*, one of her favorite childhood books. Cooper began as a sculptor and installation artist but witnessed a profound change in her work after moving in. Now she often does collage— some projects started out as plans for gardens—and her pieces frequently incorporate leaves and plants.

Both Cooper and Taggart are very involved with image and subject matter, and their art and gardening intertwine effortlessly. Their garden design evolved organically in the beginning. "Our motto was 'plants first, structure later,'" says Cooper. "Laura was the plant expert," adds Taggart, "I was the laborer." But the couple has reached parity in their planting

skills, as the success of their garden business, Cooper-Taggart Designs, attests.

A small open office/reference library on the second-floor landing separates their studios and features a window cut into the bookshelves that frames the garden—"almost like a picture," says Cooper. Her studio, complete with flower-painted computer and shelves of fabrics she uses in her collages, overlooks the chicken coop (with real chickens) and the "red" garden. It's a perfect place for their toddler Lily to play. "I've always wanted a child to occupy the garden," she says. "And the chicken coop adds a rural touch." Her paintings correspond to the vibrant colors of the red garden, which she describes as "not monochromatic but uniting, like the rich colors in a Persian carpet."

When the couple first met they were working on similar circular paintings that employed the same colors. These interconnections have only strengthened over the years. "We have a Utopian vision of life and art," says Cooper, surveying their home and studios. "Accessibility is not a bad thing."

A DOWNTOWN LOFT

The
Fred and JoAnne
Balak Studio

Most couples want to slow down as they get older, but not JoAnne and Fred Balak. Six years ago they threw caution to the wind, trading their traditional Spanish triplex on Los Angeles' affluent Westside for a downtown loft just blocks from Skid Row. "At first our friends were stunned," admits artist JoAnne Balak. "They were typical Westsiders who couldn't imagine living anywhere else. But now they look forward to coming down here to visit." Even the Balaks' son—who roams the globe as a travel photographer—was at first taken aback by his parents' midlife migration.

But after thirty years of marriage the Balaks sought more space and fewer distractions in order to concentrate on their work. JoAnne has been drawing and painting all her life. Fred, a former sales manager, wanted to leave the corporate world and dedicate himself fulltime to furniture-making. They looked at several downtown lofts before settling on a 2600-square-foot space in an ex-paper warehouse built in the 1920s. It was no-frills when they first encountered it—just four walls, three large columns and no closets

or storage space. But putting up partitions and building shelves and cabinets are no problem when there's a woodworker in the family. In no time the loft became a cozy home and studio.

JoAnne sited her painting studio by the bank of industrial windows that look out to factories and freeways. But the strong southern exposure proved too bright. Fred installed shelves above the windows so that blinds could be hung and the windows would still open. Furthermore, the shelves provide display space for the couple's art and collectibles.

The loft serves as a gallery for both artists. JoAnne's colorful abstracts share space with Fred's custom furniture, much of it created from found objects and recycled castoffs. During art openings they are able to reconfigure the space due to the wheels Fred has affixed to most of his furnishings.

The move downtown has been even more of a blessing for Fred, who, in his former life, had to work out of his garage, work that often spilled out onto the driveway. He now has a well-lighted workshop,

organized into various work stations, just an elevator ride away in the building's basement. There, his word-of-mouth business is thriving. He works in a variety of woods and styles, from country to Shaker, specializing in turning parts—such as cigar boxes, shutters, weathered doors and workbenches—into one-of-a-kind cupboards, armoires and chests.

The Balaks relish their home/studios as a constant source of creativity. "My studio is very centering," says JoAnne. "I turn off the phone and just sit in it and become inspired." Fred claims the secret to their long and happy marriage is "making things. We still get excited about the creative process. We're constantly bouncing ideas off each other."

But do they ever yearn for the leafy and well-maintained enclave of their past? "We feel safer here than we did on the Westside," says JoAnne. "We know our neighbors; people look out for one another," she continues, adding, "and when I feel tree-deprived, we go to Pasadena."

"MY SHIP AT SEA"

The Fletcher Benton Studio

For two decades Fletcher Benton has been building, renovating, remodeling and tweaking his elegant and multi-roomed studio complex in San Francisco. The artist refers to it as "my ship at sea." To be sure, the 12,000-square-foot space is a place of refuge and revelation, where Benton's art is shown to its best advantage. "The studio is about not having to fight my work," he says. "It's about composition and relation, positive and negative space."

Located in an industrial district south of Market Street, the studio appears nondescript from the outside. Once inside the door, however, a feeling of awe takes over as visitors walk into the double-height entry and reception area, all white, and light, and striking geometry. The centerpiece is a sculptural staircase that leads to a second-level bridge and mezzanine, with rooms off of it. Benton conceived the entire space around the massive eight-by-forty-foot skylight, which floods the generous areas with light. Benton's wall pieces and sculptures are highlighted in these extravagant spaces.

Off the first floor entrance area is a small office tucked under the stairs, and a guestroom complete with kitchenette and billiards table. The true heart of the studio, however, is the adjacent, sound-proofed 6,000-square-foot workshop, filled with machinery and tools of all shapes and sizes, where Benton and his longtime assistants fabricate the large-scale sculptures upon which Benton's reputation has been built. In addition to cranes, pulleys and forklifts, there is enough room to park Benton's prized 1966 Shelby racing car as well as a large truck. Light enters through tall sliding glass doors that open to an outdoor sculpture garden, and an elevator travels three flights to the slate-floored roof garden, crowned by a greenhouse and panoramic city views.

The second floor boasts a window-filled Modernist mezzanine furnished with classic Mies and Eames pieces, the walls and tabletops displaying several examples of Benton's smaller works. But perhaps the one room that most reflects the artist's spirit is his playful adjacent painting studio, where models of planes, trains and ships reflect Benton's love of toys and movement—features evident in his smaller-scale kinetic sculptures.

Nevertheless, the artist doesn't take his good fortune for granted. A former studio he owned burned down, and while this studio's completion was being delayed due to contractor disputes, Benton had to work for months in a ten-by-ten-foot space where, by necessity, he produced a series of small-scale watercolors. "I know this space is an extravagance," he says of his studio. "But it's necessary to have some extravagance in life, or else you're left with too much mediocrity."

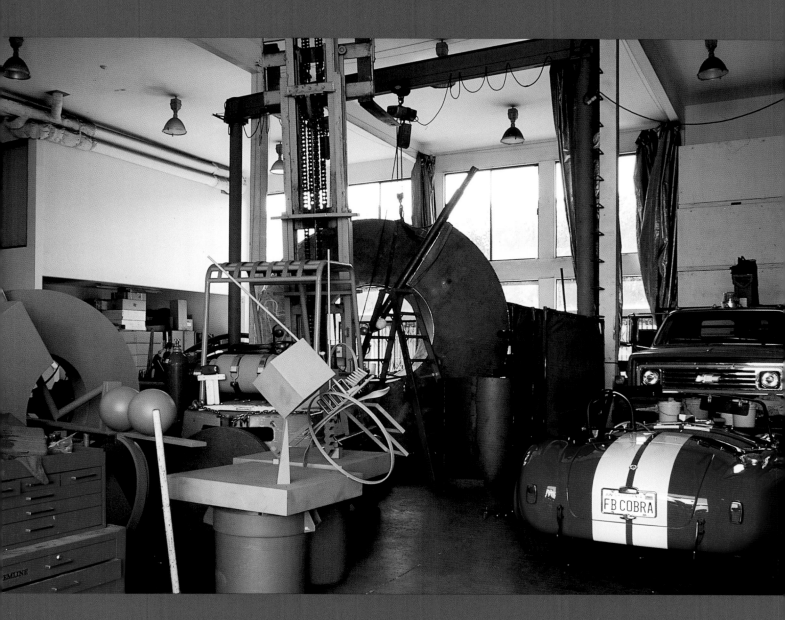

NORTH LIGHT
AND
A
POOL

The Hubert Schmalix Studio

Austrian painter Hubert Schmalix first came to Los Angeles in 1986 for an art exposition. He decided to return with his family the next year for a six-month visit. Luckily for him he had a friend who owned a luxury hotel on L.A.'s upscale Westside, so he stayed there while house hunting. Schmalix quickly realized the size of the house he needed and the city's sky-high property prices would propel him from the Westside to the more reasonably priced east. "In L.A., it's all about real estate," he laughs. Schmalix ended up in Mt. Washington, one of the city's oldest neighborhoods, which offers breathtaking views and a lively mix of cultures.

The artist could have opted for a loft downtown, but "that's not Los Angeles," he says. "Los Angeles is a house, a garden and a garage to work in." And, we should add, a swimming pool. After a successful exhibition in Austria, where Schmalix is a respected member of a loosely configured "Wild Group" of young European and American painters, he bought his

hillside-hugging lot and engaged local architects Alice Fung and Michael Blatt to draw up the plans. Schmalix's chief concerns were a large painting studio, three bedrooms (he has two college-age daughters) and a lap pool. "When you come to California you need a pool," he says with a smile. "But to swim in, not just to sit around in the sun."

Inside, however, he wanted "perfect north light," not bright sunshine, in his separate 1,100-square-foot studio, which boasts a lavender-hued exterior. To achieve that, the architects skewed the studio's saw-tooth roof so that it faced true north. They then created a series of clerestories, skylights and a large paned window to filter the north light. Almost unnoticed behind one of Schmalix's huge canvases is a tiny window that opens onto the lush arroyo seco below. "I make my own views, "says the artist. "The one outside is too distracting."

Fung and Blatt framed the house and studio with light and heavy gauge steel, which allowed for taller walls and longer spans, such as the studio's sixteen-foot ceilings. This newfound space let Schmalix expand the size of his paintings. To accommodate his large canvases, the architects also designed a sliding door next to the studio's main entrance that, when it's opened and the stair railing is removed, enables the paintings to be withdrawn.

Since coming to Southern California, Schmalix's colors have turned brighter and more playful. And, since he lives on a hill, his subject matter now includes "endless paintings of buildings." It seems it hasn't taken long for the Austrian to assimilate two of L.A.'s most cherished commodities: sunshine and real estate.

SIMPLIFICATION AND LIGHT

The Huguette Caland Studio

Huguette Caland has journeyed through three cultures and hurdled over language barriers to arrive at her elegant home and studio in Venice, California, where she's lived since the late 1980s. "You can't go backwards, that's part of changing one's life," says the artist, who was born in Beirut, where she married and raised her children.

As a young girl Caland studied the piano but turned to painting, preferring to compose her own works rather than interpret those of others. This independent spirit has served her well over the years. While still in Beirut she traded in her couture clothes for those of her own creation: caftan-like designs with an Arabic cut. "I had a difficult body so I needed to design my own clothing," she says as she doodles on one of the many white canvas smocks she wears daily. "My husband was upset but I told him some day a couturier would appreciate them."

Call her psychic. Caland moved to Paris in 1970 where, in addition to showing her paintings, she designed a clothing line for Pierre Cardin inspired by Arab dress and had an exhibition of her fashion work titled 7 Dresses. On a whim she moved to Venice in 1987 without ever having seen it. There she embarked

on yet another creation—her 5,000-square-foot house and studio. The two-story home, surrounded by a lap pool in which Caland swims every day, is like a canvas for the artist. One half is living space, the other studio, but there is much spillover between them.

On the second story a slate-floored atrium links the bedroom to the studio's loft, which features a bed and sink in case a guest spends the night. Elaborate mannequin-cum-hangars, which Caland designed to exhibit the dresses for her Paris show, stand guard over the large, clean-lined studio below.

There are no windows to distract the artist at work, but the high-ceilinged space features ample skylights as well as a series of Caland-designed rolling worktables that she can configure at will. One room effortlessly flows into another, as there are no interior doors. "My concept is simplification," she says. In fact Caland is so pleased with and productive in her surroundings she finds it hard to leave home. And the joy she feels about her adopted Venice continues unabated: "Nowhere else in the world can you have both a big city and access to a small community. And you'll never find such space in New York or Paris."

SPACE FOR
A
PHOTOGRAPHER

The Julius Shulman Studio

Whoever thinks there are no second acts in American lives hasn't met Julius Shulman. The world-renowned architectural photographer retired from taking pictures in 1986 at age 76, but he hasn't slowed down. Shulman now concentrates on writing and producing books on architectural photography, and his acclaimed photo archives are in constant demand by publishers, architectural students, newspapers, and magazines.

For more than half a century the headquarters for his two flourishing careers has been his Hollywood Hills studio, adjacent to his home. Both were designed by his close friend and respected Modernist architect Raphael Soriano. "I don't understand why more professionals don't work at home," exclaims Shulman. "Some have told me they don't want to be reminded of work when they come home. But you can still have both work and privacy," he maintains as he gazes into the tranquil courtyard that separates his studio from his home. In his hillside retreat birds, not automobiles, provide the background sounds.

Indeed, Shulman's life appears charmed. Armed with little more than a love of nature, a Brownie box camera and the rudiments of a high-school photography class (his only formal training), Shulman began shooting California's built and natural wonders. After college he returned to Los Angeles and, by chance in 1936, he met a draftsman who was working in the office of esteemed Modernist Richard Neutra. Shulman was taken to a house Neutra had built for a client in Hollywood, and the photographer shot some film. The results pleased the architect, who hired Shulman to document other works. (Over the years, Shulman shot 90 percent of Neutra's buildings.) Other prominent L. A. architects of the time, such as R. M. Schindler, Gregory Ain, and Raphael Soriano, also employed Shulman to record their projects.

The photographer's first studio was a closet darkroom in a four-room apartment. The next one was in a backyard shed. But after Shulman returned to Southern California from World War II, he purchased two acres of raw land in the hills of Hollywood as the

future home and studio he would occupy with his family. He chose Soriano to build the separate steel-framed structures that would withstand earthquakes and fires. Shulman believed that with Soriano, unlike the strong-willed Neutra, he had a partner with whom he could collaborate.

While California's Modernists were celebrating the conjunction of indoor and outdoor living, Shulman had his doubts. Unwelcome guests, like bugs, for instance, entered freely through the open sliding-glass doors. To solve the problem Shulman suggested a series of screened spaces—the precursors of today's popular outdoor rooms—including a twenty-four-by-ten-foot screened dining room, where the family took most of its meals.

Soriano also let Shulman lead the way when it came to designing his photography workshop. The forty-by-thirty-foot studio was divided into several discrete areas: a darkroom, a negative and print room, an office and a large open workspace. Situated sixteen feet from the main house, the studio has a separate entrance off the driveway, which has proved to be a godsend in recent years. With Shulman's photography conferences and the hordes of young architects and scholars perusing his archives, accessibility and parking are essential.

From his wonderfully cluttered desk—one which would give any Modernist the willies—Shulman tends to the ever-ringing phone while taking in the view of the serene courtyard. Although he moves slowly at age 93, the photographer's phenomenal memory is running at top speed, the rival of any sophisticated computer system, which he doesn't use. His impeccably maintained photo archives are arranged on card files and cross-referenced. A logbook provides a pertinent record of each project and its terms of agreement. For example, one can look up any architect's name and retrieve the accompanying job numbers. Then the person goes to either the 8 x 10 or 4 x 5 contact file and, *voila!* the necessary information is at one's fingertips. "Always make two slides," Shulman advises. "One for files and lectures and one for the client."

Now that he has retired from photography, Shulman has turned the darkroom into valuable storage space. In the main work area, a fireplace and Eames chair add a homey touch. Bookshelves are lined with bound magazines and books in which Shulman's work has appeared. And surrounding the compound are nearly two acres of verdant terraced hillside, all of which was planted or designed by Shulman.

Through the years both the photographer and his house and studio have garnered numerous awards. Shulman is an honorary member of the American Institute of Architects and a recipient of the Gold Medal for architectural photography, while his house and studio have been designated Cultural Heritage Board landmarks. (They are the only unmodified Soriano structures made of steel.) Fitting recognition for the man who became the eyes of California for the rest of the world, simultaneously putting Modernist architecture and Southern California on the map.

A FORMER CARRIAGE HOUSE

The Kate and Odom Stamps Studios

Kate and Odom Stamps met at Tulane University in the Big Easy, but their lives have become more fast track than laid-back since moving from New Orleans to Los Angeles. Odom, an architect and landscape designer, and Kate, an interior and landscape designer, decided to team up after Odom was downsized from a large commercial firm. "We began in the teeth of the recession [in the early 1990s]," says Kate of their now sought-after design business. They've never looked back. Who had the time? In addition to launching Stamps and Stamps, the couple was in the throes of overhauling a new home in South Pasadena, close to their daughter's school. "Emma said she wanted a cozy house in the woods," recalls Kate. One day after school, mother and daughter went looking for "For Sale" signs and found the perfect house at the end of an overgrown driveway. "We bought it in three days," says Kate of the former carriage house built in 1904. It had lots of bohemian charm but not much practicality. The couple began a year-long renovation to create a more formal and family-friendly home.

During the remodeling process they were not only living in but also working out of their home.

Nevertheless, recalls Kate, in spite of the stress and sleeping al fresco while roof repairs were going on, "everything fell into place." She and Odom had dreamed of maintaining studios at home, to be nearer their daughter and because of the long hours their work required.

The rudiments of Odom's architecture studio already existed—a lean-to with a concrete slab floor and heavy tile roof. To make it into a proper office they waterproofed the 175-square-foot structure and replaced the roof. "We couldn't fathom doing much else at that point," says Kate, recalling their renovation burnout. For Odom's birthday, Kate Venetian-plaster-waxed the walls a terracotta color and added an antique English architect's cabinet, studded leather files, and architectural prints.

Kate, however, was growing weary of working at the dining room table. The following year Odom designed her studio, dubbed "Kate's Castle," and located it at the end of the driveway, which, says Kate, "makes a nice terminus, and we can see who's coming." Odom's initial draft was not a great success, though. It was a squat shingled octagon Kate laughingly called a

"hut." He went back to the drawing board and produced her "carpenter's gothic" studio, adding height and removing the shingles. The result is a delightful 300-square-foot mini-castle nestled among the trees and lush foliage.

Kate's two requirements were an abundance of storage and practical working space. Hidden storage abounds under the table and work surfaces. "I skirted everything," says Kate, who also designed the chicken-wire-fronted bookcases that constitute much of the wall space. "I buy a lot at auction," she says, "so I need room for catalogs, as well as client books, fabric samples and the like. In this business you have to be organized, or the clutter will defeat you."

Working in close quarters with one assistant each has produced a familial environment that buzzes with activity. Stamps and Stamps maintains a larger office downtown to house the rest of the firm's twelve-person design staff. But it is at home where they conduct conferences, meet clients, hash out design dilemmas and hone their garden expertise. "At first all the people and activity distracted me," says Kate. "But now I couldn't imagine working anyplace else."

FIRE, EARTHQUAKE AND MUDSLIDE

The Kim McCarty Studio

Appearances can be deceiving. To reach the Malibu hilltop home and studio of artist Kim McCarty it's necessary to navigate a long and winding road. The site, with panoramic ocean and canyon views and surrounded by two acres of vineyards—the latter a project of her husband, restaurateur Michael McCarty—is heavenly. But after McCarty recounts the perils of living in paradise, *hellish* is the word that comes to mind.

The painter and watercolorist grew up in Switzerland, met her husband in college in Colorado and relocated to L.A., where she pursued a graduate degree in fine arts and Michael opened his eponymous, and now legendary, restaurant in Santa Monica. (Kim's work embellishes its walls and wine labels.) They moved to a small two-bedroom home in Malibu on their present property, and Kim kept a studio in Venice. Several years after enlarging their home, Michael planted his vineyards, and he needed a place to store grapes and other winemaking paraphernalia. Thus, a makeshift studio was born.

Kim took over part of the raw storage space for a painting studio, and the couple decided to top the structure with a tennis court. But just as Kim was getting settled into her new workspace, the McCartys moved to New York to oversee a Manhattan branch of their restaurant. They returned three years later in 1993, just months before the devastating Malibu fire that destroyed their house and 149 others. "Every home we visited on Halloween burned down," Kim recalls. Although her studio was saved, it suffered severe smoke and water damage.

Then, shortly after the family relocated to temporary quarters, the earthquake struck, causing extensive damage to their restaurant. What followed next was not a plague of locusts but devastating mudslides, caused by torrential rains. As a result of Mother Nature's fury, much of Kim's work was damaged and the couple's extensive collection of contemporary California art was destroyed. "The art and the photographs were what I really missed," says Kim. It

took the couple almost four years to rebuild their Malibu compound, during which time Kim made some changes to her studio.

She added air-conditioning and heating, and "a proper ceiling and real lighting," a combination of incandescent and florescent. Light also filters in through two walls of shaded windows that look out to the ocean and magnificent sunsets. Yet, in a comment verging on blasphemy, McCarty laments her lack of wall space. "I'd really like to board up the windows," she says sheepishly. "I live in my head, anyway."

RE-IMAGINING
A MEDICAL-ARTS
BUILDING

The Simon Toparovsky
and
Randy Franks Studios

On paper they appear complete opposites: Simon Toparovsky, the quiet, urbane East Coast Jew, and Randy Franks, the gregarious Southern Baptist from rural Georgia. But in spite of differences in age and upbringing, the two share a compatibility and commonality of vision that serves them well in their furniture and limited-edition bronzes and accessories business, Toparovsky and Franks. One reason the partners don't experience clashing egos is that before teaming up they had separate, successful careers which they continue to pursue: Simon as a fine artist—working in bronze and cast bronze—and Randy as an interior designer and space planner.

The studio in which they work was, for many years, Toparovsky's home and studio. When he first left New York and a distinguished career in hand bookbinding and one-of-a-kind art books, Simon landed in a loft in downtown L.A. Although he loved the space, he found the location too isolating. So after a few more unsatisfying living situations he bought a former medical-arts building on an unprepossessing street east of La Cienega Boulevard—an area he deems the "best microclimate in L.A., with very good light."

The building, built in 1953, was a maze of twenty examination rooms with low ceilings and no street-level windows. After Toparovsky ripped out ninety percent of the interior, he saw lots of potential—and hard work ahead. For starters, he needed skylights and new access from the outside, since the building's original entrance was through a parking lot at the rear. A portion of that parking lot is now a light-filled atrium and pond that leads to Simon's main studio—"the only room I was able to design from the ground up," he says. Its main features are double-height ceilings, four-foot-square, ground-glass skylights and stainless-steel work surfaces that are easy to clean and able to withstand high heat—two important considerations in casting's messy wax process. This is where Toparovsky worked on his commission for the larger-than-lifesize bronze altar crucifix for the

Cathedral of Our Lady of the Angels, which opened in downtown Los Angeles last year.

Toparovsky no longer lives at the studio—he has a house nearby, as does Franks—nevertheless the space retains its homey, flexible feel. It functions as gallery, studio, office and laboratory for the creative flow of ideas. "When Randy set up his office here [in Simon's former bedroom], things really started to change," says Toparovsky. "There's a velocity that happens in collaboration."

The peripatetic Franks had never been out of the Deep South until he packed up his Volkswagen and came west in 1987 with little besides a great portfolio. After graduating from art school at the University of Georgia, Franks worked on the design for Coca-Cola's world headquarters in Atlanta and helped create its corporate art collection.

Tiring of corporate design he moved to Los Angeles and became the creative director and buyer for a prominent contemporary furniture showroom. This led to the Randy Franks Studio, the design business he opened in 1993. For the next five years Franks lived and worked in the small space, which featured his favorite furnishings and accessories—all of which were for sale. It was a time of vigilant housekeeping.

Now Franks has distinct living and working environments and the room for "wide- open experimentation and freedom of expression," he says. "Friends, dealers and clients all come here, and we have this whole huge space to work out our design ideas."

A BARN
AND
A GARAGE

The Kurt Ernest Steger
and
Libby Hayes Studios

"The spirit of Lawrence Beebe is still in the barn, and his craftsmanship is an inspiration," says sculptor Kurt Ernest Steger of the man who previously occupied the huge space in Grass Valley that Steger has wrought into a 3,200-square-foot studio. The barn, built in the 1930s, and its surrounding two-acre property were part of the Empire Dairy owned by Beebe's family. When the father died, Lawrence converted the barn into a welding and machine shop for the nearby Empire Mine. "A steel welder of mythic proportions," according to Steger, Beebe lived in the barn and adjacent two-car garage until his death. His brother, a former rocket scientist, returned to the property in the 1970s and built a small, cinderblock and steel home for himself.

When Steger's partner, mixed-media artist Libby Hayes, was visiting the area with friends she came upon the listed property and found it "too incredible to pass up." Hayes has renovated several homes and welcomes a challenge. And that's just what the couple got in Grass Valley. Hayes and Steger were living in Santa Rosa and "playing with the idea of a barn," says Steger, but real estate there was too expensive. Steger,

a self-taught woodworker and furniture maker who has evolved into a fine artist working primarily in wood, immediately saw the potential in the barn. In addition to its size, it features a 25-foot-heigh ceiling, a hoist, and an eighteen-foot-wide entryway, so Steger can, as he says, "back a truck trailer into the barn to load and unload wood and materials."

To introduce more light Steger installed six two-by-five-foot skylights and built a fifteen-by-twenty-foot fine-work studio that's heated by a wood-burning stove. Steger revels at this newfound "luxury of space," which is "what sculpture is all about," he says, adding that the scale of his pieces has increased. Thanks to Hayes's tireless landscaping—most of which required a jackhammer instead of a hoe—Steger is looking forward to moving outdoors and producing site-specific pieces as well as inviting visiting artists to create works on the property.

While Steger was tackling the barn, Hayes was busy changing their home's garage into a working studio and gallery. The space definitely needed a woman's

touch after years of ownership by a bachelor. According to Hayes, she took a "very ugly cinderblock building and transformed it into a sensual, Mediterranean-feeling structure."

To effect the transformation she painted the exterior a "watered-down periwinkle blue," with terracotta touches, and added an outdoor seating area with fountain and year-round flowering plants. The new French doors bring in light and the outdoors to the gallery space and her studio. Even though Hayes admits her garage-turned-studio is still "a little dark,"

she's not complaining. It's the first proper studio she's ever had. Hayes resisted suggestions to add a drop ceiling, preferring instead to keep the pipes visible for an industrial feel. And she finds that the raw cement creates a "beautiful background" on which to display art.

In addition, her home's ample acreage and new landscaping have prompted Hayes, like Steger, to consider working outdoors more frequently and enlarging the size of her work. "Why not?" she asks. "I like to experiment. I'll try anything."

AMONG ORANGE GROVES

The John Nava Studio

244

John Nava apologizes for the crowded conditions in his studio. This is not the way he planned it to look. But then, his life for the past three years has not been what he planned either. The Ojai-based painter has been in the throes of the greatest undertaking of his career: the creation of thirty-seven larger-than-lifesize tapestries commissioned by Los Angeles' new Cathedral of Our Lady of the Angels. "It was an insane amount of work," recalls Nava, who had never done tapestries before.

Yet there's no hint of panic in this serene space, designed by the artist in 1991, four years after he and his wife moved to this bucolic valley north of Los Angeles. Before he built his studio, situated among one-and-a-half acres of orange groves, Nava worked in his garage. "Fortunately, a commission in Tokyo paid for this building," he says. In fact, a design element from Japanese temples inspired the irregular stone walkway he incorporated into the wooded stairs.

The island of Minorca, where Nava and his wife have vacationed for years, was another source of inspiration. "Right down from our house [in Minorca] was a medieval tower," he recalls. "Then, one day, farmers built a barn next to it. So I did the same thing here." Nava admits, though, that his double-height white wooden tower, with its small slot windows, ended up looking more Northern California water tower than medieval Minorcan turret. Next he attached a redwood "barn" with ten-foot-high doors.

Because the studio is located in a flood plain it was necessary to raise it three feet. Then Nava surrounded it with a low stone wall. Though the rocks are native to Ojai, the idea once again came from Minorca. To increase light he added a pair of glass doors and north-facing twelve-foot-high dual-paned windows that minimize the heat and maximize the views of the famed Topa Topa Mountains and Ojai's fabled pink sunsets. And to make sure both his work and space survive an earthquake, Nava reinforced the entire structure with steel.

His only regret is that building codes didn't allow him to construct a studio greater than 1,000 square feet. But now that his tapestry project is complete, Nava is contemplating his next creation: a second 1,000-square-foot studio to be used for drawing, photography and storage.

MEDITERRANEAN VILLA WITH A VIEW

The Miriam Wosk Studio

An ivory tower is not the place for Miriam Wosk. Her life and art intersect on all levels, and vivid color is a major component of both. A self-described "surrealist at heart," Wosk revels in the juxtaposition of objects, colors and shapes. "I express myself through my environment, which is why I love architecture so much," she says.

Wosk has been fortunate to collaborate with two of L.A.'s favorite architectural sons—Frank Gehry and, currently, Steven Ehrlich. A few years after moving to Los Angeles from New York to concentrate on her painting and collage, Wosk purchased a duplex penthouse in Beverly Hills and set about renovating it. She approached Gehry and a great collaboration was born.

A desire to be closer to the water led her to a stately street in Santa Monica and a 1927 Mediterranean villa overlooking Santa Monica Canyon. The dark and warren-like interiors were the antithesis of Wosk's aesthetic, but the home was rife with possibility. Wosk engaged Ehrlich, and the two went to work. Out went the overgrown foliage, dividing walls and small windows. Her office at the front of the house now fills with light from a newly enlarged window that overlooks the canyon. And the exterior paint exudes a warm yellow glow—"as if the sun were shining on it," says Wosk.

However, the biggest change they made was the contemporary addition at the back of the house—including a new kitchen/dining/family room area and Wosk's studio—which blends artfully with the original Mediterranean structure. The artist's previous studio was barrel-vaulted, and she requested a similar industrial, open feeling. She also wanted light, lots of it. "I just kept asking Steven for more," she says, and the architect complied, inserting half-moon clerestory windows and several skylights, as well as a sliding glass door that opens to the pool and brings the outdoors in.

The former one-story maid's quarters and the laundry room were demolished to create the current studio. The adjacent garage/guest house now serves as much-needed art storage. Wosk painted it "Frida Kahlo blue," her homage to the late artist's home and studio in Mexico City, and added a glass garage door that opens by remote and accommodates large canvases.

"Finally, I have everything I need in one place," Wosk says. "There's enough room for storage, a workroom for tools and materials, and boxes of things I use in my work. And I like the fact that I'm on ground level here. I can see the pool while I work. I've lived for many years in Los Angeles and I've never had a pool before."

A
SAN FRANCISCO ROW
HOUSE

The Tjasa Owen Studio

Tjasa Owen's expressionistic landscapes have an East Coast and European cast. "The oceans come from memories of Block Island, Rhode Island, where I grew up, and the trees are from my years living in Tuscany and France," she says. However, with the birth of her son, she appreciated the desire to be more grounded. So when Owen and her husband, Scott Kalmbach, purchased a 100-year-old San Francisco row house that had settled badly, they contacted Steven and Cathi House of House and House Architects to level out the residence and conduct a major makeover. The fifteen-month renovation returned the former duplex to a modern single- family dwelling, and converted a dark second-floor bedroom into a bright, high-ceilinged multi-use home studio.

Owen still has "a really messy studio" up the street, where she does the bulk of her painting and spraying. "In that studio it's all action," she says. "I can't think because it's such a jumble and there's no place to sit." Her home studio is where she puts the finishing

touches on her paintings. "I need to spend time with them," she remarks. She also uses this studio for sketching, collage and conducting business.

To allow for maximum light and flow, the home has no interior doors. The loft-like studio is bathed in light from large windows and doors that open onto the rear wood deck and garden. Organization is an essential requirement due to the small space. Bookshelves hold art and reference books, built-in cabinets under the desk contain necessary office equipment, and a refurbished medical cabinet displays another aspect of Owen's work—small collages that feature envelopes and all manner of old postcards and stamps. They are her tribute to the lost art of correspondence.

In addition to providing a serene haven in which to finish her art, the space allows Owen to keep close tabs on her growing son, whose bedroom is located behind the studio. And to make the space truly a family affair, it doubles as a screening room, where the entire family enjoys watching films.

ENTHUSIASM
FOR
THE TROPICS

The Robert
and
Lorri Kline Ramirez
Studio

"We took an All-American house and tropicalized it," says architectural designer Robert Ramirez, standing among palm fronds, banana-tree leaves, a lily pond and chicken coop in his Santa Monica backyard. Ramirez and his wife and partner, interior designer Lorri Kline Ramirez, have had years of experience building, renovating and restoring spaces for themselves and others.

Robert, a self-taught architect who began as a woodworker, spent six years wandering the globe, predominantly in the developing countries, learning, he says, about "the way people shelter themselves. In other words, architecture without money." Lorri, who specializes in interior finishes, cabinetry and furniture design, and space planning, shares her husband's love of travel, and the couple's enthusiasm for the tropics, from Bali to Latin America, is evident in their joint home studios. The collaboration and crossover in their work at Ramirez Design, Inc.,

echoe in their office studios, which are not segregated into "his" and" hers" spaces but rather function as "both/and."

The couple moved into their current home, which they share with their three young children, three years ago. The current architecture studio was formerly a garage, and the palapa-fringed second studio was a previous owner's woodshop. To both they added wood-beamed ceilings, skylights and plywood floors, but, according to Lorri, they still remain "works-in-progress." The second studio is a place to decide upon interiors and finishes. Lorri also calls it "inspirational." One source of that inspiration may come from the room's capuccino bar.

Reminders of their travels are everywhere. Slender pillars from Bali support the palapa awning, while an Indonesian teak door serves as the entrance to the added-on bath. The wall of the exterior shower—a signature feature in all of the Ramirezes' residential design—showcases a stone from a Balinese temple. "We can live outdoors almost year-round," says Robert. "We encourage indoor/outdoor living in our designs."

To demonstrate that they practice what they preach, their "conference room" is the outdoor space between the studios. It is covered with bamboo collected from a client's yard. "We use ephemeral materials, but the temporary seems to evolve into the long-term," says Robert of a building style he learned from the Third World. "We like to experiment with what's available. I have Native American blood. I feel very connected to the earth. Even though I'm a traveler, I need a base."

The Robert and Lorri Kline Ramirez Studio 269

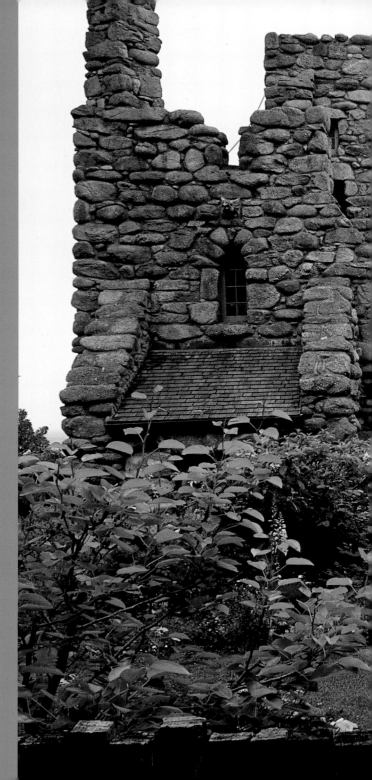

TOR HOUSE
AND
HAWK TOWER

Robinson

and

Una Jeffers' Studios

The acclaimed poet Robinson Jeffers preferred nature to his fellow man. It was fitting, therefore, that he created a home for himself and his tight-knit family on an isolated outcropping in Carmel. In 1914, when Jeffers and his wife, Una, first viewed the unspoiled beauty of the Carmel coast, south of Monterey, they had, as Jeffers described it, "come without knowing it to their inevitable place." Over the next decade the poet set about creating both his home—Tor House and the adjacent Hawk Tower—and his growing body of work on the windswept promontory overlooking Carmel Bay.

For the family's home, called Tor House after the craggy knoll, or *tor*, upon which it was built, Una Jeffers requested a small stone structure reminiscent of a Tudor barn she'd seen in England. The doors and ceilings were intentionally low to keep the interiors warm and to withstand the violent winter storms. The original two-story structure had two attic bedrooms and a main-floor guest room, living room, small kitchen and bath. Jeffers apprenticed as a stone

mason during the construction, creating his poems in the morning and his home in the afternoon.

When the main house was complete, Jeffers embarked on a more remarkable feat: the building of Hawk Tower next to the house. Named for the hawks that soared overhead, the tower, completed in 1925, was a five-year labor of love, a gift to his wife as a retreat for writing and music, and a playhouse for his two sons. He single-handedly brought the boulders up from the beach using planks and a block-and-tackle system, an amazing achievement considering some of the stones weighed as much as 400 pounds. Jeffers called the process "making stone love stone." The structure, whose walls are six feet thick, reaches nearly forty feet in height. It contains two small first-floor rooms. One, called the dungeon, is located several feet below ground level. A secret stairway leads to Una's mahogany-paneled private retreat, whose Gothic-arched windows afford commanding views. Higher still is the top of the walled turret, paved in marble, where Jeffers often observed the night sky and the powerful Pacific.

Although Jeffers's life was reclusive, distinguished visitors clambered to meet America's most popular poet of the 1920s and early 1930s, among them fellow poets Lincoln Steffens and Edna St. Vincent Millay, and celebrities Charles Lindbergh and Charlie Chaplin. In spite of the interruptions, the poet kept to his regimented habits, writing in an upper bedroom and at a nook off the dining room. In his spare time he gardened and built. Jeffers was in the midst of creating a new wing for the house—later completed by his son Donnan—when he died in 1962. The results of his labors echo in his words: "I think one may contribute (ever so slightly) to the beauty of things by making one's own life and environment beautiful." The National Register of Historic Places agreed. Today the house, tower and surrounding gardens are open to the public through the Tor House Foundation.

ACKNOWLEDGMENTS

Certainly this book would not have been possible without the collaboration and cooperation of a variety of people at every stage of the project. First and foremost, we owe a deep debt of gratitude to the owners of the studios we profiled, who withstood a barrage of questions and photographs with grace and humor: Charles Arnoldi; Fred and JoAnne Balak; Billy Al Bengston; Fletcher Benton; Huguette Caland; Art Carpenter; Robbie Conal; Laura Cooper and Nick Taggart; Alice Corning; Woods Davy; Roseline Delisle; Gregory Ghent and Xtopher Seldon; Roger Herman; Harrison Houlé; R. B. Kitaj; Sam Maloof; Kim McCarty; John McCormick; Ed Moses; Manfred Müller; John Nava; Nathan Oliveira; Tjasa Owen; Robert and Lorri Kline Ramirez; Hubert Schmalix; Tom Schnabel; Julius Shulman; Elena Siff and Sam Erenberg; Kate and Odom Stamps; Kurt Ernest Steger and Libby Hayes; Gail Sulmeyer; Simon Toparovsky and Randy Franks; and Miriam Wosk.

In addition, we thank the foundations and institutions that have so vigilantly preserved the historic studios included in this book: The Colburn School of the Performing Arts (the Jascha Heifetz Studio); The Tor House Foundation (Robinson and Una Jeffers' studios); and The Happy Valley Foundation (the Beatrice Wood Studio).

A further thank you goes to the studios' architects for their exemplary work and invaluable input: Barbara Callas; Steven Ehrlich; Frederick Fisher; Alice Fung and Michael Blatt, Frank Gehry;

Steven and Cathi House; Hank Koning and Julie Eizenberg; Robert Ramirez; and Harold Zellman.

We are indebted to those in the fields of art, architecture and design, whose insights and suggestions made our job that much easier: Julie Baker; John Berggruen; Annie Chu; Kimberly Davis; Eames Demetrios and the Eames Office; Jeanne Fenci; Patrick Foy; Shelley Gazin; Edward Goldman; Marcy Goodwin; Joanne Jaffe; Kathy Solomon; Susan Steinhauser; Mark Stock and Sharon Truax.

Special thanks go to Tisha Moloney for her unerring navigation through Northern California and to Bea Quisenberry for her inspiration. A big thank you as well to those generous friends up north for providing shelter, support and companionship on photo shoots: Kathleen Hanna, Teresa Cuatrecasas, Wendy Lichtman, Janice Purnell and Stanley Young. And last, but certainly not least, to Hugh Levick.

A&I Color Lab of Santa Monica once again demonstrated its expertise. All photos were shot with Nikon cameras using Fugi Velvia film.

Finally, our sincerest gratitude to David Morton and Douglas Curran for their problem-solving skills and their judicious editing, and to Judy Geib and Aldo Sampieri for their artful design.

—Kathleen Riquelme and Melba Levick

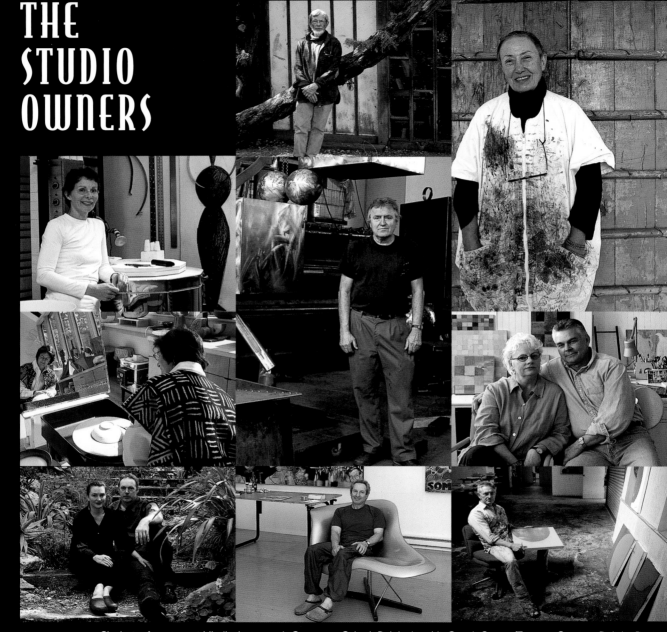

THE STUDIO OWNERS

Clockwise from top left (by last name): Bengston, Ghert/Seldon, Houlé, McCarty, Franks/Toparovsky, Müller, McCormick, Maloof

Clockwise from bottom left (by last name): Kataj, Owen, Moses, Nava, Ramirez, Schnabel, Shulman, Schmalix

Clockwise from bottom middle (by last name): Day, Stamps, Wosk, Siff/Ehrenberg, Sulmeyer, Steeger/Hayes, Oliveira